THE
POWER
— OF —
OWNERSHIP

How to Build a Career and a Business

JOHN J. BAILEY

ISBN-10: 1482639556
EAN-13: 9781482639551

The *Power* of Ownership

The Inspirational Story about a man building a career and a business overcoming many challenges and obstacles

HE FOUND you can be HONEST and succeed!

You can follow the Golden Rule and succeed!

Greed is NOT good

❖ He had no career plan or direction

❖ He was told "he was too old" to start his business

The book also features:

❖ The rise and fall of Stroh's Beer as a major brand 1975–1999

❖ A history of public relations in Detroit 1960–2012

By

John J. Bailey

TABLE OF CONTENTS

PREFACE

The ideal way to plan one's business career is to know what you want to do in your professional life while in high school and take courses toward that subject. The next step would be to establish a plan of action aimed at getting a great undergraduate education from one highly regarded university and get a master's degree from another highly regarded university. A doctorate would not hurt.

Then, plan your job career that offers you excellent experience in your field from all perspectives. This might include working in your field overseas and with several different companies or organizations. These experiences can be gained in short increments like three or five years, and it would be best if you moved around the United States, in addition to other areas in the world, to learn how different regions respond to your profession. While you are at it, learn another language or two; the business world is global.

You should plan your salary based on ten-year increments; that is, in ten years you will triple your salary, for example. You should plan your workout effort to ensure you remain healthy, and you should always be improving your personal lifestyle including buying better clothing, cars, hobbies, entertainment, professional memberships, vacation destinations, and reading better books, etc.

You must also make a commitment to life-long learning so as to keep ahead of current trends and technology. If you can determine what you want to do in life, and keep yourself motivated, you will—most likely—be successful. And luck helps, too, but you need to be ready to take advantage of it. If you do all this, you will be the owner of your professional career.

Or, you can be like the rest of us and take each day as it comes, with no real plan at all.

THE UNDERACHIEVER

This book is about a guy who was an underachiever for most of his early life. He had no plan, no direction, no inspiration, and no motivation. He was an average student getting mostly Cs with a few Bs and some Ds throughout school. He almost didn't graduate with his 1956 class because his grade in English was so low. He began his career with a weak educational foundation at best. But he liked people and wanted to be liked by everyone and always wondered what more he could do in life.

After high school he knew he needed to learn something, so he began taking night classes in the adult education program at Wayne State University (WSU), located in Detroit, Michigan. He was sure he would not be able to gain entry to a matriculating schedule in the regular college. After a year or so, he did gain entry. He didn't know what to study, and a counselor told him he needed to have a focus, so he picked public relations. He did not know why he picked this or even what public relations was. He was very lucky to have made this selection, and it was the right one for him.

The program at WSU meant he had to take freshman English, and he must have a B in the class to pass. He wondered how he could do this as he almost failed high school English and this was college.

He took the class and began reading and writing as assigned. The fear of needing a B to pass was a great motivator.

On one paper that semester, his professor wrote, "This is excellent work, even moving; you have a flair for writing." *Not me*, he thought. But he got that B in the class and with new confidence, took the next class. He still had no direction.

I carried on in night school. I knew I wanted more—always more, more knowledge, more involvement. I got into the journalism department and its advertising/public relations section. I received passing grades—even some good grades and took the next course, then the next. Of course I did not know how to type. So I went to work every Saturday for several months and taught myself—with the help of an instructional book—to become a decent typist.

All my life I have thought I was five years behind where I should be. But I always wanted more; that was the key...more. Not money, just knowledge and involvement. And I taught myself that it can be done if you keep pushing and reaching and asking "Why not me?"

I did not finish my degree program at WSU, but I came close and continued to get more responsibility at work. At that time, in the '60s, the economy was really good, and it was easy to get a better job.

I had a series of jobs between 1956 and 1975, most of them in the public relations or communication field, almost always advancing. But I wanted more and asked questions and listened and processed the answers. And I always tried to do the best job that had ever been done.

If I were to point to *one* thing that I did that helped me in the long run, it is that I *listened* and did what others suggested or told me to do...to get more...and I pushed myself to grow.

Even in organizations I joined, I always tried to do a great job leading to becoming president or the head of that organization. Just being on a board was not enough; I wanted to do the best I could and eventually to become its leader. I wanted more. As an example, in 1968–69 I was president of the Farmington Area Jaycees in Farmington Hills, Michigan and was named the Outstanding Local President in our population division in Michigan. Our chapter also won many achievement awards for community programs during my year.

I had never met any important people like state representatives or senators, council persons, mayors, and certainly not a governor. I had never presented to a large group or campaigned for anything before being active in the Jaycees. My Jaycee involvement gave me that opportunity and added to my ever-growing experiences.

My wife, Barbara, and I and our children, Karen, Beth, and Craig lived in Farmington Hills, Michigan. I was also active in the Larkshire Elementary School PTA, the Farmington Area Soccer Club (over five hundred youth soccer players) and the community itself—a suburban community of Detroit with a population of over eighty thousand. Yes, I became president of the PTA and Soccer Club, and we accomplished a lot, like getting new soccer fields for the community. I also coached a soccer team for eleven years—a sport I never played—first at the club level and then at the select or travel level, and the team did well in league and tournament play. I even got my coach's license.

I was appointed by the Farmington Hills mayor to the Parks & Recreation Commission. In that position, the Commission led the initiative to add active parks which had specific ball fields and courts and passive parks with nature trails and walk ways in Farmington Hills, where before we had one tiny park. We had to go to voters to gain tax dollars to support these efforts. We were successful. I met a lot of great people too and learned from them and began building what became a significant network.

I still had no real direction, but I kept taking what came my way. I was always wanting more, not more in a greedy sense but more knowledge and involvement. I actually believe that wanting more might be the first plan of my career. And, that plan became what I would later recognize as owning my career and later my business.

No one suggested that finishing my degree would be good. So I didn't. I was a very good public relations professional and was able to find employment and continue to get more responsibility in my career, and my family needed my time more than ever.

The following pages will show how my desire to always want more and to push myself to do the very best always helped me to build a strong career. Plus, I listened and learned from others what to do and what not to do. When I began my business, John Bailey & Associates Public Relations (JB&A), in 1996, that desire became a mantra that drove me, even possessed me—it became an *unrelenting quest for excellence.*

I will also talk about many important clients both companies and organizations I worked with over my forty-plus years working at public relations agencies. Some of their stories merit a book in themselves. I will look at the important people I came in contact with over my years in the business world. And I will talk about the community I love and always will love: Detroit, Michigan, United States of America.

I will share the life experiences and lessons learned that made up for a weak education and helped me become an important leader in my profession and achieve Hall of Fame recognition from my Public Relations of America, Detroit Chapter and even gain recognition from the forty-third President of the United States, George W. Bush.

I will share with you all the things that led me to success which can help lead *you* to success as well…adapted to your specific situation and career. The only thing you have to do is decide what you want and do the hard work to achieve success. You can do it. You own yourself and therefore your career and have the opportunity to make your career the best that it can be, and that is the theme of this book.

When I began my career, we had the typewriter. When it ended, we had the Internet, Facebook, Twitter, LinkedIn, email, texting, etc., etc., etc. What will it be like in another fifty-six years when the retirees are saying, "All we had was the Internet, Facebook, Twitter, LinkedIn, email, texting, etc."?

"I hope I shall always possess firmness and virtue enough to maintain what I consider the most enviable of all titles, the character of an honest man."

GEORGE WASHINGTON

THE DEFINITION
OF PUBLIC RELATIONS

This book is about building a career and then a business. It is not about public relations, which was the career and business I was in. The business principles I used to build my career and business will apply to just about any career and business, but just so you know, the following is the Google definition of public relations:

Public relations plural of pub-lic re-la-tions (noun)
Noun
The professional maintenance of a favorable image by an organization or a famous person.
The state of the relationship between the public and a company or other organization or a famous person.

The Public Relations Society of America (PRSA), the national organization of public relations professionals, defines public relations as follows:

"The formal practice of what is now commonly referred to as 'public relations' dates to the early twentieth century. In the relatively brief period leading up to today, public relations has been defined in many different ways, the definition often evolving alongside public relations' changing rules and technical advances. The earliest definitions incorporate the concepts of 'engagement' and 'relationship building.'"

In 2011 and 2012, PRSA led an international effort to modernize the definition of public relations and replace a definition adopted in 1982 by the PRSA National Assembly. PRSA initiated a crowdsourcing campaign, and the public vote produced the following definition:

"Public relations is a strategic communication process that builds mutually beneficial relationships between organizations and their publics."

At JB&A, we followed my definition which is:

"Public relations is the profession of communicating the right messages to the right audience(s) at the right time."

And finally, public relations is not advertising.

John proudly holding his Redford High School diploma in 1956.

CHAPTER 1

THE FIRST STEPS OF MY JOURNEY

I remember the booming times in America after WW II. During the war, Dad worked seven days, two jobs, and his "time off" was "only" working eight hours on Sunday. He worked in two automotive plants designing bomb sights and anti-aircraft guns and supervising their production and did not have to go into service. However, he was drafted in 1945 as the war was winding down, but it ended before he had to report. Even after the war, he worked two jobs for a while because of the need in America to catch up. I remember how beautiful Mom was and how great she and Dad looked when dressed up. They were young parents, she twenty, he twenty-two, when I was born. Dad graduated from the Henry Ford Trade School, we think in 1935 and received an additional diploma in die-making in 1938. This trade school education served him well throughout his career as an automotive engineer.

The years go by so fast. In many ways, I do not feel any different today than when I was thirty or even fifty. It has been good. The really early years I can't remember much; Mom, Dad, and I lived in several places in Detroit from 1938 until 1943. Then came 12292 Woodmont (I was about ages four to twelve); then in about 1950, 17551 Greenview (ages twelve to twenty-five), both in Detroit.

Sister Beverly Jill was born in 1945 when I was seven. My schools were Coolidge Elementary, Tappan Middle School, Emerson Grade School (first graduating class of 1952), and then Redford High School (class of 1956). I was a bored student who did well only when motivated. I remember Mrs. Ruth S. Burch, from Coolidge Elementary, who liked me, and Miss Cyretta Morford, from Redford High School, who didn't like me.

My mother and father were Marjorie Eleanor and Joseph Edward. Marjorie was always there and Joe was always working. They were honest, hard-working people...where I got both traits. They were simple people who loved their family and stayed in Detroit. They believed in and taught me that "doing what is right at all times" and "if you don't have anything nice to say, don't say anything," are the way to live.

Those were the guidelines I began with and lived my entire life. I followed the "doing the right thing" credo almost always. But not saying anything unless I had something nice to say was harder and I may have broken that rule a few times along the way...even in this book...but only when I thought it was important to "doing the right thing."

Sister Beverly Jill and I were not close in the early years because I was so much older. I was on my own by the time she was in high school. But later she and husband Ronnie and my future wife, Janet, and I became close, even though they live in Orlando. Thanks to social media, we remain in constant touch with each other.

Dad passed away far too young at seventy-one in 1987 after a successful career as an automotive engineer first at the Ford Motor Company, then at General Motors from where he retired. He did not get to see me create and build my business. He did see my success on the Stroh's beer account at Anthony M. Franco, Inc., Public Relations (AMF, Inc.) and was very pleased. Mom lived another twenty-four years and missed her Joe every day. They had been married for fifty years when he passed. She was very proud of my success in business. Marjorie and Joe were inseparable during their many years of marriage. I dedicate this book and my career to them. They gave me just what I needed.

SELECTIVE SERVICE SYSTEM

LOCAL BOARD NO. 48
Wayne County
14705 Grand River Avenue
Detroit, Michigan
(STAMP OF LOCAL BOARD)

August 18, 1945.

Order No. 3227

Joseph Edward Bailey,
12292 Woodmont,
Detroit 27, Michigan.

Dear Sir:

Please disregard Order to Report for Preinduction Physical Examination on August 21, 1945.

Yours very truly,

WAYNE COUNTY LOCAL BOARD NO. 48,

Mary E. Pulford

Mary E. Pulford, Clerk

PG:HY

Joseph Bailey's notice that he did not have to report for his pre-induction physical to enter WW II.

The neighborhoods in northwest Detroit were just fine for a young boy. We had lots of ball fields and play areas and even an ice rink that the City of Detroit flooded during the winter. There was also lots of construction going on...new homes, schools and businesses...that we kids could play in.

I remember huge elm trees and the smell of burning leaves in the fall...you could do that then. As kids we'd make piles of leaves to jump in or hide in and jump out at passers-by.

I played a little organized hockey in Detroit Recreation leagues and even played at Olympia Stadium in 1952 and 1953, then home of the NHL Detroit Red Wings. One Saturday, the Red Wings were practicing and invited us to join them on the ice (we were in uniform waiting for them to finish practice and watching in awe). We played with them for a few minutes, and I even took a shot on Red Wing goalie Terry Sawchuk and was lightly "crashed" into the boards by "Terrible Ted" Lindsay... both are NHL Hall of Fame players. I also played baseball and football whenever I could. We never stopped playing sports. In baseball I was a good left-handed hitter but had trouble catching. In football, I could run and catch, and in hockey, I could really skate. I was almost always the fastest skater on the ice. But for the most part, I never played organized sports.

My best friend on Woodmont St. was Bobby Hunter. Bobby and I played all sports together; he was my age almost exactly. There was a neighborhood bully who was much bigger and a couple years older than us, who used to push us around, take things from us, and beat us up. One day, as the bully approached us, I got down on my hands and knees behind him, and Bobby pushed him over me. We pounced and proceeded to beat *him* up for a change. He never bothered us again. I didn't realize it then but, I had taken ownership of this situation and made something different happen for me and my friend.

Lessons Learned: *Stand up for yourself. Any two of us is better than any one of us.* **(Little did I know that forty-plus years later that would be an important feature of my business.)**

I remember some things about WW II even though I was just over seven years old when it ended; at least I think I do. I think I remember my dad pulling the car off the road and both Mom and Dad crying upon hearing the radio announcement about the attack on Pearl Harbor. I remember my dad working so much that I hardly saw him. I remember spending a lot of time with my mom, which was really nice. I remember running around the neighborhood crashing pots and pans together in celebration when the wars ended in Europe and then Asia. I remember my uncle Johnny, my mother's brother, sending letters home from Tokyo as a member of the occupying troops. I also remember him bringing me a hand-carved black bear from Japan that I still have. I remember the growth in America after the war and how good things were, at least from a kid's point of view.

I meandered through those years. I would have benefited from more direction. I graduated from Redford High School in 1956—a C student. But I always stuck my nose in somewhere and looked for something else and was always trying for more and asking "Why not me?" I didn't know it then, but those were two of my secrets—listen and keep digging. I was active in numerous school organizations, always trying for more.

My best friends in high school were Dale Barr, who had a successful career teaching at Olivet College in Michigan, Robert Beauchamp, who went on to success in the real estate field, and Jerry Gillen. My girlfriend was Nancy Moore. I was crushed when Nancy broke off our relationship just after high school, I think because she was too good for me and went to the University of Michigan while I floundered. I can understand that now. I have not seen Jerry or Nancy since just after high school.

I was also friends with C. Michael Armstrong, our class president, star athlete, and great-looking guy. Mike was voted "Most Likely to Succeed." He had a hugely successful business career culminating in his being named Chairman and CEO at AT&T.

My two career goals at that time were to make $20,000 a year, which was then a lot of money, and I wanted *everyone* to like me.

Sister Beverly Jill also went to Redford High School, got married, moved to Florida, became a nurse, and raised a great family of two sons and a daughter. She is way smarter than me. She is now enjoying twelve grandchildren. Her goal is to retire to live in a home at or near the beach by the Atlantic.

Lesson Learned: *Stick your nose out there and get involved; you learn a lot and gain invaluable experience.*

CHAPTER 2

MY FAMILY

Family is first, always and forever. Family is what you do every-thing for. Never lose that perspective. Family is your foundation. It was for me then, and still is.

Barbara Ann Stines and I were married in 1963 and lived in an apartment in north-west Detroit in 1963 through June 1964. We then moved to Farmington Township, Michigan. Our home at 30215 Stockton was a wonderful family home. We paid a whopping $16,290 for the home, but could not afford the larger model which cost $17,100. Imagine me in "the burbs" with a mortgage and large lawn to mow as part of one of the first waves to leave the city of Detroit and to move to Farmington Township, an upscale suburb. Our children Karen, Beth, and Craig came along in 1964, '67, and '70, and the years from 1965 to 1992, when I moved out, flew by. The kids, and now their families, were and are the most important part of my life.

The kids and their early lives were so much fun—respecting, encouraging, supporting, disciplining, and loving them. I was deter-mined to be part of their lives all the way, something my dad could not do.

Many years we had an ice skating pond in the backyard which got lots of use...even I got out on the ice. One year we had about thirty inches of snow in one week, and the snow banks surrounding the ice pond were piled over the fence. It was beautiful, especially at night with the flood lights on.

From photography to music and bands and gymnastics, to soccer and more soccer—it was a beautiful time. We vacationed "up north" in Traverse City, Michigan went to movies, had many sleep-overs, and more. Of all the things I have accomplished in my life, helping raise three beautiful grown-ups is the *greatest*. I am so proud of what they have become. They are strong people fighting the fight to get ahead and never giving up. My time with them is the most beautiful memory of all. I have always said that the title I am most proud of in my life is: *daddy*. Grampa is pretty strong too.

Lessons Learned: *Know what is important. Your family is your foundation. Family is first.*

All three kids went to Farmington Harrison High School. One of my goals was to provide them with a college education, something my parents could not provide for me. When Karen went to Michigan State University (MSU) in East Lansing, Michigan, I was a proud father. Imagine me, the meanderer and college drop-out, with a daughter at a major university. Then Beth followed to MSU. It was tough to accomplish financially, but by then my career was moving nicely at AMF, Inc. where I served as head of its largest account, The Stroh Brewery Company, and I finally had some direction—by accident maybe—and I was ready. When Karen was a junior in high school, we had no idea how we would finance her college education, let alone that of Beth and Craig. We did not have the money. By the time Karen enrolled at MSU, somehow we came up with the money as my career was finally—at age forty-four—beginning to take off. Barbara worked weekends at Sears, and that was a huge help.

The girls were excellent students and very involved in lots of things, and even though there were some bumps—like car crashes—they always made me happy and proud. They both graduated from MSU in four years. Karen went on to get her MA in community counseling and Beth her MBA and teacher's certificate. Along the way they both provided the ultimate—grandchildren, when Justin and Brandon from Beth, and Timothy and Kevin from Karen, were born. What a thrill. They were followed by Craig's two sons, Colin and Griffin. (Yes, we have six grandsons and Briley Kate Weed our lovely great-granddaughter.)

Craig was a good student and received his Bachelor's degree from Central Michigan University (CMU). He was a tremendous soccer player. He excelled in soccer at every level. It was an honor and pleasure to watch him grow from a little kid to Honorable Mention All-American in '90 and All-American in '91 plus two-time All MAC Conference at CMU. In 1990 he was the eleventh leading scorer in the nation with 16 goals and 11 assists and finished 18th in national scoring in '91. He would likely have established a CMU career record for goals, but for a career-ending injury in the first game of his senior year. He ended his college career with 34 goals; the school record was and is 42. To both of us, the injury and what it meant was crushing. I remember thinking, why us, why now? The record would have been nice, but health is most important, and we still have all those great memories, and a school record is not the most important thing in life. Living life is.

Once while I was watching the CMU versus Oakland University soccer game at OU, a very braggadocio father whom I did not know was telling me about how great his son was and that he received a full soccer scholarship at OU, which had a strong soccer program at that time. He went on and on about how many colleges recruited him, etc. I did not say one word. CMU eventually won the game 1–0 on a goal scored by my son. The father asked as we parted, does your son play? Yes, I said, for CMU. I did not tell him that Craig had scored the only goal of the game to defeat his son's team, but it was sweet enjoyment for me.

We are also very fortunate to have two great sons-in-law and a great daughter-in-law. Ken Morrison is the best construction professional I have ever known and a wonderful person. He is married to Karen. Marty Weed, retired U.S. Marine Captain, is married to Beth. We are all very proud of Marty and his twenty-three-year Marine career. Susan Morgan Bailey is a nationally recognized leader in corporate health promotion and is like a daughter to us. She and Craig are married.

In those years my best friends were Laura and Del Van Vliet, Barb and Thom Seabolt, Chris and Bill Dzyngel, and the kids on Craig's teams and their parents.

Unfortunately, Barbara and I drifted apart and were divorced in 1988. When I sold 30215 Stockton in 1992 after twenty-eight years, the kids were out of college and on their own. It had been a wonderful home for the Bailey family. But times change and the family grows up. Then the good times in a home and the love shared there become memories, and it is OK to move on. We all did and kept the memories and the love alive.

Lesson Learned: *Sports are fine, but they are not as important as living a good life, and building yourself into the best person you can be.*

CHAPTER 3

MY COMMUNITY

I have mentioned my desire to keep learning and meeting people and gaining experience. To help me accomplish these goals, I joined the Farmington Area Jaycees. This was a very active group that had as two of its goals to serve the community and to provide leadership opportunities to its members. Boy, was I excited. I could learn more about leadership and practice public speaking. I could meet important people like a mayor, city council member, and maybe even a state representative. I was a member of the Jaycees for seven years and was very active. I even got to coauthor the word script for two musicals that were performed by the seventy-five-member chapter plus wives, and I wrote hundreds of press releases in those years. The organization gave me what I had hoped for and more. During my years as a member, I chaired many projects, and I served as a board member and president in 1968–69. I did indeed meet important people, culminating in the occasion when, as public relations chairman for the Michigan Jaycees, I met then-Michigan Governor William G. Milliken in 1969. That was a huge big deal for me.

In 1969 The Farmington Area Jaycees earned "outstanding chapter in the state of Michigan" in our population division, and I was fortunate to receive the award for outstanding local president (out of more than two hundred) presented by the Michigan Jaycees. The awards were not as important as the work we did in the community and the experience I gained as the leader of that chapter and of young men.

Farmington Township became the City of Farmington Hills in 1973. The Farmington Area Jaycees supported this vote and actively worked to support its passing.

My involvement in the Jaycees and coaching Craig's soccer team for eleven years led me to be involved in the Farmington Soccer Club serving nearly six hundred youth soccer players. I served that organization as president from 1982 through 1985. During this time we were successful in finding and building three new soccer fields for our kids. These involvements lead me to a mayoral appointment as commissioner of the Farmington Hills Parks & Recreation commission from 1983 to 1991. During my years on the commission, we gained community support to construct several new active parks with specific ball fields and passive parks with nature trails and walkways for use by residents of Farmington Hills.

I can't move on without mentioning Larkshire Elementary (Grades K–6) where our kids attended school from 1969 until 1981. Larkshire's principal, James A. "Al" Lanigan, was a wonderful man who loved his "little apples," as he called the kids. Mr. Lanigan is one of the greatest people I've ever known. I was not alone in that thought, as the Farmington School Board renamed the school James A. Lanigan Elementary upon his retirement. I was active in the Larkshire PTA serving as its president. Mr. Lanigan called me Mr. Sports Night because I chaired the annual "Sports Night" at Larkshire several times.

Lesson Learned: *Dig in, work hard at everything you do, and it will pay you back.*

CHAPTER 4

MY EARLY CAREER

Right after high school in 1956, I took a few adult education classes here and there looking to keep learning. But I had no plan. In high school I had done well in architectural drawing, so I took a course in architecture at Lawrence Institute of Technology, now Lawrence Technological University. In the lab class, the final exam was to create and mix cement in a container at your work station. We were graded on how high the cement mix would stand. When I turned my container over, the mix ran off the table to the floor. I'll never forget what the instructor said: "Mr. Bailey, perhaps you should try another field." That ended my attendance at Lawrence Tech and architectural studies.

A year later, I enrolled at Wayne State University (WSU) night school where, over the next eight years, I completed 161 of 180 credits required to graduate but all of the requirements in my major. I found I loved literature and reading and that lead to my reading passion that I will reference later. In high school I was a horrible writer and hated reading but WSU changed that for me. Miss Morford would be proud. Completing science was—and is—in the way of my degree. If only I had found the encouragement to study science. While at

WSU, my counselor asked what I was going to major in. I told him I had no idea. He said I must make a choice. So I said, public relations; I didn't know why. I was so lucky. I had selected the right profession for me. This is a critical point. A person needs to know what she or he is good at. My subconscious knew that I would be good at public relations, and again luckily, I had the temperament and aptitude for it.

Lesson Learned: *Good Luck is good.*

Burroughs Corporation 1956–1969

Burroughs was a major Detroit employer and the manufacturer of adding machines and computers. It was later acquired by Unisys Corporation and moved to Pennsylvania. After I graduated from high school, my dad got me an interview at Burroughs. It was easy getting a job in those days, the economy was booming after the war, and education was not an issue. If you didn't like the job you were in, you could simply go out and get another one.

At Burroughs my career and life were without direction early on, but I had a job and always looked for more and did not take no for an answer. I was always the youngest person in a meeting, and they never listened to "the kid." I was in the mail room first—right out of high school—then the architectural drafting department, and then public relations, at the end of my years at Burroughs. I was the news editor of the *B-Line*, an internal newsletter serving the Burroughs International division—my first writing job. My architectural drawing experience gave me a sense of page balance and straight lines that benefits me to this day.

Burroughs was two blocks from WSU, which was very convenient as all my classes were after work. I also could study at my desk and even taught myself how to type at my desk at Burroughs.

In 1956 my starting annual salary at Burroughs was $2,620.80, or $50.40 per week, I was eighteen years old. At thirty-one I left

Burroughs for Chrysler and an annual starting salary of $7,800. WOW!

Chrysler Corporation 1969–1971

I went to the Chrysler engine plant on Mound Road as "plant editor," writing all copy for their four-page monthly publication. Management was not concerned that I had not finished my degree; in fact, they didn't even ask if I planned to continue my studies. The Mound Road Engine plant was a great experience in "life" as I worked on each of the three shifts one week per month to gather plant news. Not all, but a few of the workers—especially on the night shift—drank, smoked pot, partied hard, skipped out to the bar across the street, and yet still managed to produce engines.

One beautiful summer Friday morning—which happened to be pay day—some of the workers whom I had befriended told me to not be around at lunch time. So I scheduled a meeting at HQ in Highland Park, Michigan. After paychecks were distributed at the plant, a lead hammer miraculously and "accidentally" dropped into the main production line, breaking the line, and shutting down all production. All workers were sent home about 11 a.m.—on a beautiful summer Friday—with 95 percent pay for that day. Aw shucks.

Later that year I was called to the Highland Park HQ. I was doing great work, fit in nicely with everyone, and was often complimented by management, I thought I was going to be promoted to a larger plant with an eight-page monthly newsletter; instead, I got laid off. This was the 1971 economic downturn, and I was a victim.

Lessons Learned: *Bad things can happen to good people even when you are doing a good job. It is tough out there. Anyone can be cut.*

Special Note: During my career I was laid off four times. Each time I bounced back and was better off than before. *You can too.*

BBDO (Batten, Barton, Durstine & Osborn) 1971–1973

BBDO is a national advertising agency which at that time had a public relations component to serve its advertising clients. One of BBDO's largest clients was the Dodge Division of Chrysler Motors. Here I had the good fortune to work with two tremendous and very experienced public relations professionals: John Richard Hurley, who was in his late fifties, and Glenn Campbell (not the singer), who was in his forties. Even with the writing experience I had so far, it was not enough; I was still a bad writer. John Richard and Glenn were very patient and helped me tremendously in this category. I also was introduced to publicity, as John Richard was a genius publicist with Glenn not far behind. John Richard had been a successful Hollywood publicist before arriving in Detroit, gaining publicity for movies and movie stars. He had not even finished high school, but to overcome his lack of education, he studied the dictionary daily learning new words. He had the largest vocabulary of anyone I ever knew. John Richard taught me the art of publicity. I used that skill I am sure hundreds of times throughout my career. While I was at BBDO, one of my publicity photos for Dodge that I supervised for the 1974 Detroit Auto Show made the front page of the *Detroit News*—a huge success for me, the client, and the agency. I learned publicity for publicity's sake from these two pros and got a little better at writing.

Little did I know that twenty-seven years later my firm would be doing the public relations for the entire Detroit auto show, which in 1989 would become the North American International Auto Show.

The '60s and '70s were the times of heavy drinking and smoking in our society, with long lunch hours and womanizing. It was common for executives—mostly men—to have four to six drinks at a long lunch. The folks at BBDO were no exception, and I saw a lot of staggering in the halls after lunch. I was too junior and therefore not privy to these activities, so I watched. I could not drink that much anyhow. Watching the television show *Mad Men* reminds me of everything that happened in those days.

One day after lunch, a bunch of executives, who had gone out for a typical long lunch hour, gathered in Hurley's office. Someone was showing off a pistol that he was carrying. The gun went off and the bullet slammed into the wall of a nearby office. I was scared to death but not hurt. I got up and left for the day. I heard nothing more about that incident or my afternoon off.

A few months later, John Richard Hurley called me into his office—I was doing well and was probably getting a promotion, I thought. I was all smiles and excited with anticipation. Mr. Hurley told me the client, Dodge Division of Chrysler Motors, had cut its public relations budget, and I was being laid off. I was stunned. But he said he saw a great future for me in public relations; however, not at BBDO. He called his good friend Beverly Beltaire, founder and president of PR Associates, a significant public relations agency based in downtown Detroit's Penobscot Building, and got me an interview. I was hired and started the Monday after leaving BBDO with six weeks' severance pay in my pocket. We used the extra money to buy living room furniture. And this was my first job at a public relations agency.

Lesson Learned: *Work hard and try hard; you can make good things happen from bad.*

PR Associates 1973–1974

Beverly Beltaire was a tremendous public relations professional and pioneering woman in business in Detroit and was the "first woman chairperson of many organizations including the Detroit

Regional Chamber of Commerce," which later became the largest local chamber of commerce in the United States. Bev is in the Public Relations Society of America (PRSA) Detroit Hall of Fame.

I also met Ray Eisbrenner at PR Associates, where he was executive vice president. Years later Ray started his own public relations agency which would be the model for my firm. I learned more from Ray and Beverly during my stay at PR Associates. Ray gained my life-long respect as an ethical businessman, public relations professional, and family man. Ray is also in the PRSA Detroit Hall of Fame.

I took part in—in my opinion—the worst publicity stunt of all time, certainly of my career, while at PR Associates. We did some public relations work with Weight Watchers, and they were opening a new office on 12 Mile Road in Southfield. The publicity gimmick we used to supposedly attract positive media attention was to string a row or ribbon of real animal fat across the front door of the new building. The Weight Watchers' president, would "cut the fat" as a symbol of their services. It was July and *hot*. And the fat began dripping, attracting hundreds of flies. It was disgusting.

Thompson Brown Realtors 1974

One of my mistakes in my career was leaving a good job at PR Associates, for one I did not understand, for a little more money, a nice title, and a shorter drive to work. I was to be director of Public Relations and Advertising and assistant vice president for this large local realty company that also constructed new home communities in the region. I really felt I was moving up in the world. Their HQ was in the City of Farmington Hills, and they knew me from PR Associates and my Farmington community activities. It was fun the short time it lasted, but I eventually got laid off there, too. I wasn't feeling too good about myself after being laid off from three of my last four jobs.

Lessons Learned: *Don't be tempted by a title and a little more money. Stick with a good thing until you are ready to move on. Sometimes things happen for a reason. Keep working, trying, and learning, and never give up.*

The Spinal Column 1974–1975

I was released from Thompson Brown on my birthday in 1975. They didn't understand public relations and did not think they needed the services I could provide. There I was, a man with three kids and a wife, out of a job again. A friend of mine from the Jaycees, Chuck Williams, knew the publisher of *The Spinal Column*, a western suburban Detroit weekly newspaper. Chuck told him what a strong leader I was. I got the job and I needed it. I was in charge of getting the newspaper out each week, and my understanding of straight lines and page balance was hugely beneficial.

I eventually lost my position there too and began immediately to look for a job back where I belonged, in public relations. And I was getting really tired of other people making decisions about my future.

Lessons Learned: *Always keep pushing yourself to learn and grow; don't look back. And do what you do best.*

CHAPTER 5

MY REAL CAREER BEGINS

<u>My Years at Anthony M. Franco, Inc. (AMF, Inc.) 1975–1989</u>

AMF, Inc. was founded in 1964 by Anthony M. "Tony" Franco and grew into one of the largest full-service public relations firms in Michigan, if not the largest in those years. It was growing and was "the place to be." Tony hired me for $11,000 a year as an account executive. I knew Tony from PRSA, and we had always said that we would work together some day. The timing was right, and I was very pleased to be back in public relations where I belonged. My first day on the job at Franco, my car broke down on the way, and I was several hours late. You can imagine how scared I was to walk in the door. Remember, this was before mobile phones.

In the spring of 1976, I had been at the firm a few months when my mentor, Bill Luddy, who was head of The Stroh Brewery Company account at AMF, Inc., called me into his office. He said the Stroh account (brewers of Stroh's beer) was growing, and he thought I'd fit in well with the staff there and the Stroh family itself. The Stroh family owned the company and ran its day to day business. The Stroh Brewery Company was a strong regional brewery with two excellent products that had outstanding reputations. The products were Stroh's Bohemian Style Beer (America's Only Fire-Brewed Beer) and a brand it had acquired in 1964, Goebel beer. Stroh's beer was sold in eleven states and Goebel in seven states. In 1972 Stroh had entered the top ten for the first time, and in 1973 it sold four million barrels of beer in seventeen states and was the eighth-largest brewery in the United States.

Several Stroh family members were active in the company, including: John W. Stroh, Chairman; Peter W. Stroh, President; Eric W. Stroh, Assistant Vice President of Marketing, and Gari M. Stroh, President, Stroh's Ice Cream Division. *

*Note: **The name Stroh is used in reference to the family and company while Stroh's is used in reference to Stroh's beer and all its products.**

The family and company were major players in Detroit and southeast Michigan, sponsoring events such as the Detroit Power Boat races and the J. L. Hudson's/Stroh's fireworks on or near the July 4th holiday (now the Ford Fireworks presented by Target). The company had also been radio or television sponsors of Detroit professional sports teams including the Lions, Tigers, and Red Wings. The company was poised to expand nationally and with new products. AMF, Inc. was in the enviable position to be able to grow with the iconic Detroit brewing company.

Bill asked if I would be interested in joining him on the Stroh account. I had worked on a few Stroh projects with Bill and was thrilled and honored, plus I drank Stroh's beer. He went on, "There are two trips on the July 4th weekend: one to San Diego, California and one to Houghton Hancock, Michigan, in the Upper Peninsula," where the International Guts Frisbee tournament was being held with Stroh's beer the sponsor. Stroh's beer was also a sponsor of a music concert in San Diego. He asked me to guess which trip I would be going on. I said "I love northern Michigan." He laughed. I did too, and that began the most wonderful, fun, educational, exciting years I had experienced to that point in my career.

While at the "Guts Frisbee" tournament, I experienced the first of many crises situations while serving The Stroh Brewery Company. The night before we left for the event in Northern Michigan (I was able to take my family), some six hundred miles from our home, the J. L. Hudson's/Stroh's Fireworks had taken place on the Detroit River front, between Detroit and Windsor, Canada. Approximately 1.1 million people attended the event, and that night, there were two incidents of purse snatching and fighting. The media called me, as Bill was in the air on his way to San Diego. I calmed them down by suggesting that the two incidents, even though more than anyone wanted, were not bad when considering there were over a million people viewing the display. I suggested they check other cities around the United States with over a million people to see how many crimes had been committed in the same time period. That gave them some perspective, which softened the story. I also assured them that Stroh's, even though disappointed, would continue its sponsorship.

The next spring I travelled on one of the greatest business trips I ever experienced. Bill and I went to Florida to visit with the management of two of the professional baseball teams Stroh was sponsoring to discuss promotional activities. I spent four days in meetings with the Cincinnati Reds management and talked about promotions. Then I spent four days with the Chicago White Sox management, where I met the inimitable White Sox owner Bill Veeck (Veeck, as in wreck) and popular Hall of Fame radio/TV announcer Harry Caray. The meeting with Mr. Veeck was at 10:30 a.m. before a 1 p.m. baseball game, where we would meet Mr. Caray. Veeck was called "the Barnum of Baseball and the game's most magnificent maverick." We walked into the conference room at the hotel where the While Sox were staying and Mr. Veeck asked me, where's the Stroh's beer? I went out and bought two cases of Stroh's which barely lasted until game time. On the trip I also managed to visit the Detroit Tigers' spring training camp. All in all, I saw about twelve Reds, White Sox, and Tigers' spring training games. I know you won't feel sorry for me...I got sun poisoning during the trip.

Later that year, Bill and I traveled to Cincinnati along with Stroh marketing executive Art Erickson. As part of their planned corporate expansion, Stroh's beer had increased its radio professional sports sponsorships beyond the Detroit teams and had added the Cincinnati Reds baseball team and later the Chicago White Sox and had hoped to add the Pittsburgh Pirates. At that time, the Cincinnati Reds had won two World Series and had a very strong regional radio network, which was appealing to Stroh. Stroh's beer had sponsored the Reds for three years in the mid '70s, and we were in town to present its proposal for another three years. In the new contract proposal, Stroh had significantly increased the money and promotions (we were there to discuss the promotions) over the first three years. The Reds general manager said, "We love you guys and would love to keep working with you. You've been a great partner. But Anheuser-Busch has offered us well over three times what your offer is." There was no decision. The Reds were negotiating with one of their star players—Pete Rose—on a new multimillion dollar contract and had use for the additional cash. Stroh's beer would no longer be the radio sponsor of the Cincinnati Reds. This was a sign of things to come.

In the 1970s and early '80s, Stroh's beer sponsored numerous events in northern Michigan, from sailboat races and events to auto racing to snowmobile racing. Stroh's beer sponsored the Triple Crown of Snowmobile racing held in January and February with 250-mile and 200-mile oval track races in Traverse City and Alpena and concluding with the International 500 Mile Race in Sault Ste. Marie the first week of February. Attending these events to help promote the sponsorship and sending the results to media around the state was work, but the events were always fun, even if they were always on the weekends and I was most often away from the family. I also got to work with M. John MacLeod, Stroh Sales Promotion Manager at these events, and we became great friends.

Stroh had no public relations professionals on its internal staff. AMF, Inc. served as its public relations department. In the early years of the relationship, in the late 1960s and early '70s, AMF, Inc. reported weekly bowling scores to the media from the Stroh's and Goebel professional bowling teams and the annual press release on beer production for that year. But Stroh was poised to push itself into the world as a major player and to fight its way into the competitive world of Anheuser-Busch, Miller Brewing, Schlitz, Coors, Pabst, et al. From the mid-1970s onward, AMF, Inc. grew into supporting Stroh Corporate, market expansion, brand management, sales promotion, and all aspects of the brewing company's business.

In 1976 The Stroh Brewery Company opposed the Michigan Bottle Bill, formally or legally the Michigan Beverage Container Act. This was the state-wide initiative in Michigan to establish deposits on beer and soft drink bottles and cans. The deposits were to be five cents on refillable containers and ten cents on non-refillable containers. The aim was to clean up Michigan's highways of discarded beverage containers. Stroh was opposed to the bill because they believed that it was a hugely expensive solution to a problem that could be solved for far less money. It was Bill Luddy's plan, approved by Stroh executives, for him to support the Stroh efforts opposing the issue while I supported the marketing efforts for the Stroh's beer brands and market expansion. By the way, the bottle bill passed by a wide margin and has been law ever since.

Bill retired in 1977, but before that he taught me a lot about the beer industry, the Stroh staff, and the family. He always said, "Never forget the Stroh family in any decision you make." Bill also taught me that anything can be done...it might cost a lot...but anything can be done. Here's an example: One-time Detroit Mayor Coleman A. Young had agreed to participate in a noon news conference we were hosting at the Strohaus hospitality center. His office called at 7 a.m. that morning and informed us the mayor was in Milwaukee and "would not be able to attend because of a lack of an appropriate flight." Bill called me and said, "We need to get him here…let's figure something out." We brainstormed and came up with two ways we could get the mayor to our noon event…and one worked—we were able to get him a ride in a navy plane that was travelling to Michigan. Bill was a retired Navy officer and had the right contacts. This option did not cost a thing as the plane was already scheduled to visit Michigan.

On a sad note, Bill Luddy died a few months after retiring at age sixty-one, never getting a chance to enjoy retirement. He had touched the hearts of everyone who knew him and gave me my start with Stroh. I wish he could have seen how the Stroh account grew and changed at AMF, Inc. I also wish I could have known him longer.

Lessons Learned: *Stick with what you know best; we are mortal; anything can be done…it might cost a lot but…anything can be done. Listen to those above and below you in the "org chart." But the important thing is to always listen.*

CHAPTER SIX

MY STROH YEARS

I was responsible for providing public relations services to The Stroh Brewery Company from 1975, and when Bill retired, I became head of that account at AMF, Inc. until 1989. Stroh became the largest account at AMF, Inc., with annual billings growing from a few thousand per year to over $500,000 per year at its peak. In those days AMF, Inc. reportedly billed in the $2 million to $4 million range and may have even attained the $5 million level as reported to us by Tony Franco.

In my time Stroh grew from two brands in eleven states to twenty-two brands in fifty states. These years were career high-lights and gave me the opportunity to do just about everything in the public relations world. They were great brands and we expanded them all over the country. Unfortunately, Stroh could not compete long-term with the big breweries like Anheuser-Busch (A-B) and Miller. I advanced to executive vice president at AMF, Inc. One former Stroh executive said, "Your experience with us was like you earning an advanced degree in public relations."

It should be noted that my comments and opinions about The Stroh Brewery Company are from my position as a person very close to the company and its people and management. Many weeks for almost fourteen years, I would work fifty or sixty hours with Stroh executives on Stroh business and was often thought of as a Stroh employee by outsiders. One year I travelled on Stroh business trips during twenty weekends, which did not fit well at home. But my office was at AMF, Inc. and my support team to Stroh was at AMF, Inc., and I planned our public relations support of Stroh at my AMF, Inc. office. Stroh management made its decisions, and we were called in to implement communication surrounding those decisions. With a few exceptions, we were not part of the decision process. To help confirm dates or the sequence of events for this book, I met with or talked with numerous former Stroh executives. These executives were a huge help in providing timing and opinion of what happened at The Stroh Brewery Company in those very critical times for the company.

I mentioned earlier that when I started working with The Stroh Brewery Company, it had two brands in eleven states. Over my years we expanded—mostly through acquisition—to twenty-two brands in fifty states, and Stroh's beer was the flagship brand and leading seller, and marketing needed to keep it that way. Stroh's beer had like a cult following outside its marketing area, much like Coors beer did. People would carry a case of Stroh's beer and trade it for a case of Coors beer and the other way around when traveling around the United States.

To help introduce Stroh's beer and its products to new states, we had special events across that state, including sponsored "fun" events like concerts, rodeos, tennis tournaments, tough man contests, tractor pulls, sports sponsorships, beauty pageants, etc.; whatever fit the culture of that state. But we also had the business story to tell to the business pages in the major cities of each state as to why Stroh's beer was coming and what it was bringing with it.

Our job was to get publicity in the local communities in each state for the events and sponsorships and to get Stroh executives interviewed at all events and for business focus stories. This led the way for the brand advertising that would follow and gave the "new brands" much more "top of mind awareness" than if only advertising was used.

During one state introduction, I drove to North Carolina in a caravan of Stroh's beer eighteen-wheel trucks leaving Detroit and gaining publicity along the way. It was great fun, but it also made a great visual and served to introduce Stroh's beer to consumers in those states between Michigan and North Carolina.

When introducing Stroh's beer in the state of Texas, Chris Lole, Stroh Vice President of Corporate Planning and Development, and I used the Stroh-leased Lear Jet and flew into six cities across that great and huge state, gaining for Stroh and Lole six to ten business pages, and radio and TV interviews in each city while the sponsored events were going on; one featured a few of the Dallas Cowboy Cheerleaders and several Cowboys players.

The introductions were mostly very successful. On May 23, 1983, John H. Bissell, vice president of marketing for Stroh, sent me a memo congratulating us on the successful intro of Stroh's and Stroh Light beers in Texas. Bissell said:

"Having recently seen the stack of newspaper publicity on the Stroh's/Stroh Light Texas introduction—I want to extend congratulations to you on a spectacular achievement!

The well-placed, lengthy, and positive articles in key newspapers speak for themselves in terms of their value in establishing Stroh's in the Texas market. Perhaps we'll give up all those expensive TV GRP's and simply send you back to Texas every month." (GRP is Gross rating point, is a measure of television advertising performance.)

Stroh's beer introduction in Georgia was also very success-ful. In both Georgia and Texas, we conducted the Stroh's Rose of Georgia and the Stroh's Rose of Texas campaigns. They were both beauty pageants where women from across both states competed to be named the "Stroh's Rose of Georgia" or the "Stroh's Rose of Texas." They were fun events and got beer drinkers across both states involved in the nomination and voting process. One former Stroh marketing executive told me; "Stroh's sales in Georgia took off and reached a 10 percent share after sixty days and a 17 percent share after six months." It is unfortunate this sales level could not be maintained.

AMF, Inc. also provided public relations services to historic cor-porate events, such as the introduction of new products like Stroh Light in 1978 and super premium Signature beer in 1983 and all other new or acquired brands.

The Stroh Detroit Plant Closing

In 1985 the company closed its iconic Stroh brewing facility located in downtown Detroit near Interstate I75 and Gratiot Avenue. This was a huge blow to the local economy and image of the Detroit community. The old brewing facility built in 1912 with some of the earliest buildings on the site dating to the 1860s was the most expen-sive brewing facility to operate in the country and was land-locked and could not expand. Our challenges at AMF, Inc. were:

1. To deliver the message that Stroh was not leaving Detroit or Michigan and would remain a major player and employ-er in Detroit for years to come, even though the plant was closing. The plant had been there since 1912 but the first cellars were located on the site in the early 1850s though the first Stroh brewery, then named Lion, was not completed until 1867 on the site. The brewery had been expanded

many times over the years. But the facility had become the least efficient brewing plant of all brewing companies in the country. And the Stroh acquisitions had given them several newer and more efficient brewing facilities and lower production costs.

2. To minimize negative responses from business and government leaders and if possible, have these leaders say something positive about Stroh.

3. To communicate that The Stroh Brewery Company would do everything in its power to help workers find new career paths, if not another job.

In one planning meeting regarding the details of the plant closing, about twenty of us were sitting in the huge boardroom at Stroh with company officers, lawyers, investment counselors, and other senior consultants. I was the least important person in the room—I know I made the least money. They were talking about closing the plant on February 14, 1985. I got up my nerve to say...you can't close it that day. They all looked at me like I was from outer space. What could this lowly public relations idiot be thinking...we are in charge...I could read this on their faces.

Why? They demanded.

"That day is Valentine's Day, and the newspaper headlines would likely read, 'Another Saint Valentine's Day Massacre,'" I said. (This is in reference to the St. Valentine's Day massacre in 1929 where seven mobsters were murdered in Chicago in a prohibition era conflict.) At the very least, it would be a lousy Valentine's gift to husbands, wives, and sweethearts.

I got all the support I needed when Peter said, "John is right." We chose another date.

Lesson Learned: *You must speak up when you have a point to make.*

All twenty corporate officers had input into the closing decision and development of an official statement explaining it. They were all assigned to contact Detroit and Michigan "thought leaders, business leaders, and politicians" on the morning just before the announcement with the details. Our job was to ensure as much as possible that the key community leaders heard about the closing before it aired and had the important information as to why the plant was closing so they would be better prepared to offer insight if or when asked by the news media.

Peter Stroh met with Detroit's mayor and key business leaders, while others met with Michigan's governor and called state and federal officials. More than two hundred opinion leaders learned about the closing from Stroh itself, rather than through news media. Same-day meetings were held with union officials and brewery workers. Calls and meetings were completed before the February 8, 1985 11 a.m. news conference, when the May 31, 1985 closing was made public.

Here is what Michigan's Governor James Blanchard, Detroit's Mayor Coleman A. Young, and Detroit Chamber of Commerce President Frank Smith said in the Detroit media:

> "If they don't believe there's any set of circumstances under which the brewery can be salvaged, there's no sense in misleading the community, city, and state," said Governor Blanchard.

> "The job and economic loss to the city from the shutdown will be more than offset by Stroh's growing investment along the city's riverfront. I am disappointed…it's not an easy thing to take, but it's not all negative. It does not mean that Stroh is abandoning Detroit. There's a consolidation on a manufacturing level, but an expansion on an administrative and real estate level," said Mayor Young.

"Stroh is still a Detroit institution...it is headquartered here. Its name and corporate personnel will be a continuing part of the Detroit scene," said Frank Smith.

Helping Stroh workers:

On April 15, 1985 we hosted another news conference to cover the plan to help as many as possible of the nearly one thousand employees who would lose their job to begin a new working life. Stroh provided outplacement services, resume writing counseling, career and life counseling, educational services, and more. This was to last for months after the closing. Our public relations team had presented a plan to promote this aspect of the closing and kept record of how many workers found work...the percentage of those who wanted to work—some went back to school, some stayed home, and some retired—was very high. And the key message that Stroh was not leaving Detroit was well received by the market-place. It was a great effort by everyone inside Stroh and the AMF, Inc. team. We continued to update the community of the progress employees were making in finding jobs. And this effort lead to considerable positive media coverage in local, trade and some national media.

In talking with Roger Fridholm, who was president then, about this book he mentioned how pleased he and other top management at Stroh were with the fact that their plan to help workers was published as a Harvard Business Review Case Study in 1987.

These were the days before computers, so to make sure all media got the message that "Stroh was not leaving," I produced a photo of the original brewery, the building imploding, the empty lot, and the architect's drawing of the new Brewery Park, all on the same page. The key media all received this photo. They couldn't miss the fact that the company was not leaving, could they? That site and the new modern building on it is now the home of Crain Communications, publishers of many publications including *Crain's Detroit Business*, *Automotive News*, and *Advertising Age*, to name a few.

Just over a year after the Stroh plant closing, I received this note from Stroh vice president Bill Weatherston.

Dear John:

Listening to Peter's speech before the Women's Economic Club last week when he mentioned the plant closing a little over a year ago now, reminded me of the tremendous PR success that we continue to enjoy relative to that closing. You made believers out of both Chris Lole and me that even the most difficult public relations situation can be planned for, carefully choreographed, and effectively presented.

You know, we did a great job.

Sincerely,

Bill

The following pages are copies of the original documents including the press release announcing the plant closing, Peter Stroh's remarks at the press conference, and other facts about the company, its employees and Stroh's beer. All were prepared at the time of the plant closing.

FOR: THE STROH BREWERY COMPANY

Contact: John Bailey

STROH DETROIT PLANT OPERATIONS
TO BE PHASED OUT THIS SPRING   FOR IMMEDIATE RELEASE

        DETROIT, Feb. 8 -- The Stroh Brewery Company announced today
that it will phase-out operations at its Detroit, Michigan brewing
facility this spring. The plant, located on Gratiot and I-75,
currently employs approximately 720 hourly and 170 salaried workers.

        Peter W. Stroh, chairman and chief executive officer of the
company said, "This was one of the most difficult decisions we have
ever made. We have studied the situation and various alternatives to
closing the plant and we are positive this decision is best for our
entire company. Closing this plant is a necessary step which
strengthens our company for the future and for our remaining 5,500
employees nationwide and our 900 wholesalers.

        "Of course, our corporate headquarters, including over 750
employees, will remain in Detroit at our current River Place
development. Our faith in the city of Detroit and the state of
Michigan is and will remain at the same high level as it has in the
past. And, we plan to continue to play a major role in the future
growth and development of both the city and state."

        Stroh Properties, Inc., a Stroh land development company, is
presently in the construction and development of the 30-acre River
Place property on the Detroit riverfront.

                            -more-

Christopher W. Lole, vice president-corporate planning and development, explained, "The company is involved in a very competitive non-growth industry with approximately 50 million barrels of excess capacity, which represents 22 percent of total industry capacity. It was determined, after an exhaustive study, that operating the Detroit plant was considerably more expensive than our company average and a great deal more expensive than our most efficient facility. We also analyzed the cost of making the Detroit facility competitive and found that to be impossible due to physical lay-out and space consider- ations."

Art Tonna, executive vice president-operations, has informed the employees and their respective unions about the phase-out and will begin working with all parties to negotiate the necessary plant shut-down agreements. "It is our desire to work with the unions and employees for the benefit of all concerned." Tonna said.

The firm Jannotta, Bray & Associates, Inc. will handle outplacement for all salaried and hourly workers.

The company also announced that future redevelopment of the property will be turned over to Stroh's development company, Stroh Properties, Inc., which will be forming an advisory panel to consult on the future of the site. The advisory panel is expected to be comprised of local government and business leaders.

All Stroh products will be brewed at six other brewing facilities located around the country in Allentown, Pa., Winston-Salem, N.C., Memphis, Tenn., Longview, Tex., St. Paul, Minn., and Van Nuys, Calif.

Based on industry estimates for 1984, The Stroh Brewery Company is the third largest brewing company in the nation.

-30-

(CHRIS LOLE, VICE PRESIDENT OF CORPORATE PLANNING AND DEVELOPMENT)

GOOD MORNING. MY NAME IS CHRIS LOLE. I'M VICE PRESIDENT OF CORPORATE
PLANNING AND DEVELOPMENT AT STROH. IN A MOMENT, I'LL BE INTRODUCING
PETER STROH, OUR CHAIRMAN, FOR AN ANNOUNCEMENT. BUT ALSO WITH US
TODAY AT THE TABLE, TO THE RIGHT OF PETER, IS ROGER FRIDHOLM, OUR
PRESIDENT AND CHIEF OPERATING OFFICER, AND TO THE RIGHT OF HIM IS
DICK LODATO, WHO IS OUR SENIOR VICE PRESIDENT OF ADMINISTRATION.
THE FORMAT OF OUR CONFERENCE TODAY WILL BE AN ANNOUNCEMENT FROM
PETER FOLLOWED BY A QUESTION AND ANSWER PERIOD, WHEN YOU'LL BE ABLE
TO ASK QUESTIONS OF MR. STROH, MR. FRIDHOLM, MR. LODATO OR MYSELF.
IN THE INTEREST OF BEING FAIR AND EQUITABLE TO ALL, THERE WILL BE NO
INDIVIDUAL INTERVIEWS FOLLOWING THIS CONFERENCE AND WHEN YOU ASK THE
QUESTIONS, WE'D APPRECIATE IF YOU WOULD IDENTIFY YOURSELF AND THE
ORGANIZATION TO WHICH YOU WORK. NOW, WITHOUT ANY FURTHER ADO, I'D
LIKE TO INTRODUCE MR. PETER STROH.

-1-

(PETER STROH, CHAIRMAN)

GOOD MORNING, EVERYBODY. I'M PLEASED YOU CAME OVER TODAY, BUT I'M
NOT VERY PLEASED WITH WHAT I'VE GOT TO TELL YOU. THE REASON FOR
THIS GATHERING IS TO ANNOUNCE THAT THE STROH BREWERY COMPANY WILL BE
PHASING OUT OPERATIONS AT OUR DETROIT PLANT DURING THE SPRING OF
THIS YEAR. THE DECISION TO CLOSE OUR 135-YEAR-OLD FACILITY ON
GRATIOT AVENUE HAS BEEN THE MOST DIFFICULT AND PERHAPS THE MOST
IMPORTANT DECISION WE'VE EVER HAD TO MAKE. WE'VE STUDIED THE SITUA-
TION INTENSIVELY, WE'VE CONSIDERED EVERY CONCEIVABLE ALTERNATIVE
TO CLOSING THE PLANT, AND WE'RE POSITIVE THAT THIS DECISION IS THE
BEST FOR OUR ENTIRE COMPANY. CLOSING THIS PLANT IS A NECESSARY STEP
TO STRENGTHEN OUR COMPANY FOR THE FUTURE AND FOR OUR OTHER 5,500
EMPLOYEES -- 750 OF WHOM ARE HERE IN DETROIT.

THE COMPANY IS INVOLVED IN AN INDUSTRY WHICH IS NO LONGER GROWING
AND WHICH HAS SUBSTANTIAL EXCESS CAPACITY. THE CLOSING OF THE
DETROIT PLANT WILL PERMIT US TO OPERATE OUR REMAINING PLANTS AT
THEIR FULL RATED CAPACITY AND AS A CONSEQUENCE TO COMPETE MORE
EFFECTIVELY. UNFORTUNATELY, OUR DETROIT PLANT IS OUR OLDEST AND
LEAST EFFICIENT AND NO CAPITOL INVESTMENT, CONCESSIONS, OR ANY
COMBINATION OF THESE COULD TRANSFORM IT INTO A SUFFICIENTLY VIABLE
BREWERY FOR THE LONG PULL, IN THE CURRENT INDUSTRY ENVIRONMENT.

-more-

I WANT TO EMPHASIZE VERY STRONGLY THAT OUR NEED TO CLOSE THE PLANT
IS NOT A DETROIT PROBLEM. IT IS NOT A WORKMEN'S COMPENSATION PROBLEM.
IT IS NOT A UTILITY CHARGE PROBLEM. IT IS JUST A PROBLEM OF A PLANT
THAT IS VERY, VERY OLD, GEOGRAPHICALLY CONSTRICTED AND NO LONGER
COMPETITIVE WITH THE MODERN FACILITIES WHICH SO DOMINATE OUR INDUSTRY
TODAY.

THE TIME HAS COME TO TAKE THIS VERY DIFFICULT ACTION AT OUR LEAST
EFFICIENT FACILITY SO THAT WE CAN REMAIN A COMPETITIVE FORCE. TO
REMAIN COMPETITIVE WE MUST REDUCE OPERATING COSTS, INCREASE PRODUC-
TIVITY AND MAINTAIN AN IMPROVED PRODUCT QUALITY. CLOSING THE DETROIT
PLANT IS A NECESSARY STEP TOWARDS ACHIEVING THOSE GOALS. THREE
YEARS AGO, WHEN WE WERE FACING THE QUESTION OF WHETHER SCHLITZ WAS
GOING TO ACQUIRE STROH OR IF STROH WOULD ACQUIRE SCHLITZ, WE KNEW
THEN THAT IF SCHLITZ HAD ACQUIRED US THERE, PLANS WOULD HAVE CALLED
FOR THE IMMEDIATE CLOSING OF THE DETROIT PLANT AND OUR CORPORATE
HEADQUARTERS AS WELL.

I WANT EACH OF YOU AND ALL DETROITERS TO KNOW THIS HAS BEEN A VERY
DIFFICULT DECISION FOR THE STROH FAMILY. WE'VE BEEN AGONIZING OVER
THIS SITUATION FOR SOME TIME NOW. TO THE EXTENT THAT WE DO ANYTHING
TO JEOPARDIZE OUR ABILITY TO SUCCEED IN THE BREWING INDUSTRY WE ALSO
JEOPARDIZE OUR ABILITY TO REMAIN A VIABLE CORPORATE CONTRIBUTOR TO

-more-

THE REVITALIZATION OF THE CITY OF DETROIT AND THE STATE OF MICHIGAN.
AS YOU WILL SEE IN THE NEWS RELEASE YOU'VE BEEN HANDED, OUR CORPORATE
HEADQUARTERS WITH 750 EMPLOYEES WILL REMAIN HERE AT RIVER PLACE.
AND AS MANY OF YOU KNOW, WE'VE RECENTLY COMPLETED A NEW STATE OF THE
ART ICE CREAM FACILITY AS THE HEADQUARTERS OF OUR ICE CREAM OPERA-
TIONS JUST ACROSS THE BREWERY, ADJACENT TO THE STROH HOUSE.

FURTHERMORE, WE BELIEVE THE DEVELOPMENT THAT WE'RE ENGAGED IN HERE
AT RIVER PLACE, TOGETHER WITH THE OTHER RELATED DEVELOPMENTS OF
A.N.R. AND MICHCON AND SOME OF THE DEVELOPMENTS WHICH WILL TAKE
PLACE--WITH WHICH WE HOPE TO BE ASSOCIATED IN THE NEXT FEW YEARS--
WILL RESULT IN MORE JOBS FOR THE CITY THAN ARE BEING LOST AS A RESULT
OF THE CLOSING OF OUR PLANT. THE FACT THAT OUR HEADQUARTERS WILL
REMAIN IN DETROIT AND THE FACT THAT THE COMPANY WILL BE CONSIDERABLY
STRENGTHENED AS A RESULT OF THIS PAINFUL MOVE WILL ENABLE US TO PLAY
AN EVEN STRONGER ROLE IN THE FUTURE OF DETROIT
AND OUR STATE. NOW, I BET YOU ALL HAVE AN AWFUL LOT OF QUESTIONS
AND I'D BE GLAD TO TRY AND ANSWER AS MANY OF THEM AS I CAN.

-more-

THE STROH BREWERY COMPANY
FACT SHEET

HISTORY

1850   Bernhard Stroh moved to Detroit and established a brewery
            at 57 Catharine.

1867   Stroh builds a larger brewery at 331 Gratiot.

1912   Construction was begun on the current brewing facility at
            Elizabeth and Gratiot.

1914   The brewery is ready for operation; fire brewing process
            installed.

1915   The brewery is expanded with a new garage added.

1936   The first modern storage cellar is completed.

1950   Stroh builds the largest single span bottling plant in the
            world and adds more storage cellars.

1958   A warehouse is constructed on the site.

1984   Production capacity is 7.2-million barrels of beer.
            Present production is at the 3-million barrel level
            currently employing 720 hourly and 170 salaried workers at
            the Detroit brewery.

BREWERY DIMENSIONS

The brewery is located on 40 acres and contains one million square
feet of plant, office and warehouse space.

BRANDS PRODUCED IN DETROIT

Stroh's, Stroh Light, Signature, Goebel and Goebel Light

CLOSING RATIONALE

To reduce operating costs; increase productivity and maintain product
quality.

ADDITIONAL INFORMATION

Outplacement services will be available for both hourly and salaried
workers.

```
                    DETROIT STROH BREWERY PRODUCTION
                              FACT SHEET

   Year                                           Barrels

1850-1918                                      11,000,000
1918-1933 (prohibition)                        -----------
1933-1950                                      10,129,066
1950-1960                                      16,045,940
1960-1970                                      23,171,074
1970                                            3,275,846
1971                                            3,676,283
1972                                            4,231,400
1973                                            4,645,833
1974                                            4,364,555
1975                                            5,133,370
1976                                            5,765,328
1977                                            6,114,424
1978                                            6,328,599
1979                                            6,015,246
1980                                            6,161,255
1981                                            6,193,714
1982                                            6,311,000
1983                                            5,298,000
1984                                            4,091,000
```

Year	Brewery Employees	Payroll
1983	1,050	$31 million est.
1984	900	$40 million est.

Year	Federal Excise Tax	State Tax
1983	$47 million est.	$5.4 million est.
1984	$47 million est.	$4.7 million est.

Additional Information

Total Brewing Capacity at the Detroit plant= 8,659,128 barrels.

One barrel is equal to 31 gallons or 13.778 cases.

Total production for The Stroh Brewery Company's seven brewing
facilities in 1984 equalled 23.9 million barrels.

THE STROH BREWERY COMPANY
100 River Place
Detroit, Michigan 48207
(313) 446-2000

Products:

The nation's third largest brewing company produces eleven brands of beer with six line extensions including: Stroh's, Stroh Light, Signature, Schlitz, Schlitz Light, Schlitz Malt Liquor, Old Milwaukee, Old Milwaukee Light, Goebel, Goebel Light, Schaefer, Schaefer Light, Schaefer Low Alcohol, Silver Thunder, Piels, Piels Light, Erlanger and Primo.

Brand Managers:

Stroh's - Mike Jaeger
Schaefer -Ed Kopecky
Signature -Mike Mitaro
Old Milwaukee -Charles Powell
Schlitz -Tom Noble
Erlanger -Jovan Jovanovski
Piels/Primo/Goebel -Ed Kopecky
Schlitz Malt Liquor/
Silver Thunder -Michael Porter

Breweries:

Location/# of Employees
Allentown, Pennsylvania/705
Winston-Salem, North Carolina/518
Memphis, Tennessee/650
Longview, Texas/450
St. Paul, Minnesota/425
Van Nuys, California/450

Can Plants:

Location/# of Employees
Chatsworth, CA/250
Fremont, OH/300
Longview, TX/400
Oak Creek, WI/365
Winston-Salem, NC/600

Employees:

7,000 nationally
  650 corporate employees

Production:

23.9-million barrels in 1984
24.3-million barrels in 1983
22.9-million barrels in 1982

Wholesalers:

A national network of 1,128 distributors. A total of 843 distribute the premium flagship brand Stroh's and Stroh Light.

Established:

In 1850 by Bernhard Stroh

# # #

-0437M

<u>DETROIT HOURLY EMPLOYEES - SUMMARY OF 729 PEOPLE</u>

1. 125 are skilled trades: machinists, electricians, operating engineers, firemen/oilers.

2. Of the 604 non-skilled workers:

   239 are under 40

   20 are 62 or over with 10 or more years of service and
   can retire with lifetime medical benefits.

   approx. 200 are Brewery Workers under age 62 who will sever with over
   $50,000 cash available through their retirement plan, and
   paid vacation and personal days - (of the 200, 150 are
   over 55).

   approx. 10 other non-skilled personnel should be eligible to retire
   under their respective severance pay or pension plans
   with substantial benefits.

   approx. 135 (+10) remain who are non-skilled whose total severance
   package will be below $50,000 in value. But, of these,
   70 will get $25,000 - $50,000.

The Explosive Years at Stroh

Everyone I talked to in preparation for writing the Stroh section of this book referred to Peter Stroh, the company president who would become CEO then chairman, as a master strategist and visionary. Peter knew the beer industry thoroughly—it was in his blood—and he had great expectations for his company to play a significant role in the industry. He knew, as he often said, "We must either grow or go." The company fought to survive but eventually could not. Some of the former Stroh marketing executives said it was not possible to support twenty-two brands—and later even more—with nation-wide marketing, especially for a private company. But it was more than just money.

Peter Stroh also knew that the alcoholic beverage industry must promote responsible consumption. He encouraged the entire industry to do this, and at AMF, Inc., we worked closely with Stroh on responsible drinking message campaigns sponsored by Stroh, one of the first alcoholic beverage companies to move in this direction.

Peter knew that for Stroh to survive against the "Big Boys" at A-B and Miller it had to reduce costs while growing, and to do both, he believed the company had to hire new, well-educated and strategic-thinking professional staff just like A-B and Miller were doing. One of Peter's first moves was to hire Roger Fridholm as vice president of strategic planning around 1978. Roger was brought on to be, as one former Stroh executive said, the "change agent" from the old school hands-on Stroh management to new school Stroh strategic management. Fridholm, with his masters of business administration (MBA) from the University of Michigan, had worked in strategic planning at McKinsey & Co. in Chicago, one of the leading global management consulting firms, and most recently at Heublein Inc. or Heublein Spirits, an American producer and distributor of alcoholic beverages and food throughout the twentieth century. Just over a year after his arrival, Roger was appointed president of The Stroh

Brewery Company. Peter Stroh, a Princeton graduate, became CEO. Roger and Peter made a good team, as Peter was the visionary, and Roger was the one to make the strategic plan to get things done and in some cases, do the dirty work like layoffs. John W. Stroh, then in his mid-80s, became chairman emeritus.

In 1979 a study of the brewing industry was conducted for Stroh by a major eastern US consultancy. The purpose was to confirm what Stroh management already suspected, that Stroh could not survive long-term in the beer business against its strong competition. The study showed this to be true even if Stroh performed well because the economies of scale were against the company and favored the much larger A-B and Miller. But Peter and the Stroh family must have agreed to try to save the brand that carried its family name for over 130 years anyhow, and they asked Roger to get it done. .

The study also showed that Stroh should move out of the alcoholic beverage business and into another food product field. This recommendation was not popular and was ignored...for a while.

This began a new era at Stroh and what I call the "attack of the MBAs." Roger—with Peter's approval—began hiring graduates from universities with the best business schools who were indeed well-educated and were supposedly strategic thinkers. John H. Bissell was hired in 1979 as vice president of marketing to establish brand images for the brands through advertising. By then, Stroh Light had been introduced. Bissell was not an MBA but was a Yale graduate and came to Stroh with national strategic marketing experience with marketing juggernaut Procter and Gamble (P&G), marketers of consumer goods such as Crest, Tide, Bounty, and Pampers among many other products, and more recently, Frito Lay.

Bissell said that when he joined Stroh, he..."inherited a traditional beer marketing organization of mostly long-term beer men (note *men*) with little or no experience in any other business. Most were competent in what they were supposed to do: execute beer promotions with wholesalers. There was no capability in strategic marketing including brand management, advertising, media planning, and marketing research. The corporate culture was: 'Do what I say, don't make waves and you'll be well paid and you'll have a lifetime job.'"

This sentiment was very similar to the sentiment at A-B as presented in the 2011 book, *Dethroning the King; the Hostile Takeover of Anheuser-Busch*, by Julie Macintosh. The major difference was that A-B was many times larger than Stroh with lots more cash.

In the competitive market where A-B and Miller were upgrading strategic planning and hiring outside brand management talent, the lack of strategic planning at Stroh was a recipe for failure. So, they changed too.

Brand Management

Bissell introduced the brand manager concept at The Stroh Brewery Company with the new folks—most of them MBA's—at the head of the brands. I am not an advertising expert, but I always thought Bissell did an excellent job at Stroh and from the promotions and increased responsibilities he received in his Stroh years through 1991, Stroh management thought so too. In fact, after Bissell had been with the company for several years, one of the most senior and most respected "old guard" managers complimented Bissell by telling him he *was* a "beer guy" after all, the greatest compliment a "new guy" could receive.

Initially Bissell brought in four MBA outsiders plus a couple business consultants and hired one of them, Hunter Hastings. The marketing department was about fifty people when Bissell joined Stroh. He terminated several marketing employees and a few more later. After the Schlitz acquisition and the significant increase in brands and budget, fifteen more marketing professionals were added. The Stroh advertising budget was about $85 million annually, and that increased to $137 million after Schlitz. A lot of money for Stroh, but a fraction of what A-B and Miller were spending to market their products.

On a personal note, I always got along with all the MBAs. I tried hard to bridge the gap between the new and old guard managers, including Hunter Hastings. The only problem I had with Hunter was that he was a professional ice hockey fan, as I am. His favorite team was the New York Islanders who were winning several Stanley Cups in those years, as the champions of the National Hockey League. My team, the Detroit Red Wings, was always in last place and was laughingly called by Hunter, the "dead things." We parted company before the Red Wings drafted super star Steve Yzerman and began winning their Stanley Cups in the '90s and 2000s.

Some of the MBAs listened and learned the beer business and with their education and strategic thinking did a great job. But the arrival of these folks created a we/they situation between the new-comers—who the old guard thought did not understand the beer business—and the old guard; conversely, the newcomers thought the old guard were not as sophisticated as they needed to be to grow con-sumer products nationally. Some of the newcomers did not fit in and they moved on, some not soon enough. Once I was in a meeting with the new Stroh's beer brand manager and several other marketing executives that had been at the company for years. We were talking about the target Stroh's beer drinker. One of the old guard Stroh marketing employees began talking about the "target consumer as a man who stops on the way home from work a couple times a week and buys a twelve-pack of beer. He goes home and drinks all or most of the twelve-pack that night and does this more than once a week." The new MBA brand manager looked around the room and said, "Do you mean there are people who drink that much beer?" We were all shocked and knew at least that brand manager could not survive at Stroh. He didn't.

This new/old conflict caused distrust between the new MBAs and the old guard marketing managers. One side said, we are going to grow these products nationally, while the other side said, you can't take care of our babies like we can. Situations like the twelve-pack example added fuel to the smoldering fire.

Roger himself was brilliant and had many great ideas. It was his leadership that led the way for this regional, family-owned brewing company to go national and compete with the giants. Peter Stroh knew this had to be done to try to save Stroh's beer, and Roger was the guy he thought could do it.

Stroh Wholesalers Struggle

Stroh management and Roger lost the trust of the Stroh wholesalers though—these are the people who distribute the beer to retailers around the country. One top executive said that Roger and Stroh management thought Stroh should have far fewer wholesalers than it did. Even though they were right, that did not make the wholesalers feel good at all. After the Schaefer and Schlitz acquisitions, Stroh had almost as many wholesalers as A-B and Miller who produced far more beer than Stroh, and this was something that would lead to problems ahead. And the Stroh wholesalers were not happy about the money they were making with the smaller Stroh's brands, while the A-B and Miller wholesalers were rolling in money. Because the Stroh wholesalers were not making a lot of money, they did not have much to spend on local marketing, either. There were some markets where Stroh's, Schlitz, Goebel and Schaefer beers were being delivered by four different wholesalers where A-B and Miller each had one. This issue was a major concern to Stroh, Roger, and the wholesalers. Some say this lack of trust between the wholesalers and the very top Stroh management and the problems this caused could have been the major reason for the eventual fall of Stroh's beer as a major brand. It certainly didn't help.

Roger was strong-minded. He had his opinions, and that was that no matter what. One time he asked me and John MacLeod's opinions on the hiring of a promotional team that I knew well. I told Roger that I did not think he should hire the group as they would not represent the Stroh family well, and I did not trust they would do the job promoting the brands that we all wanted. I told Roger that if he hired them, in less than one year they would sue Stroh, Roger, and me for lack of support even though they would not do their job. Roger was impressed with my honesty but hired them anyhow. Yes, before one year was up, they did attempt to sue, but the case was dropped. It was a mistake and waste of my time and Stroh money.

Another time Patrick J. Fox, a wonderful man who had been at Stroh for years as a sales manager and worked with its wholesaler body, was "retired" and left the company before he wanted to. The company gave Pat a farewell party and a wonderful gift of international travel tickets. But Pat had a strong relationship with the wholesalers, and they loved him and wanted him back. They put up such a fuss that Pat was brought back. After he returned Pat told me, "John, my wife and I had a great trip and vacation and now I am back making more money than ever." I was told that this retirement was the decision of a Fridholm guy and had Roger's approval. This move added to the distrust the wholesalers had. It was not a good situation.

Lesson Learned: *It is good to listen and mix the old with the new. Always listen. Respect everyone.*

Purchase of Schaefer and Schlitz

In 1981 and '82, Stroh made several acquisitions, including east coast-based Schaefer beer and the much larger Schlitz beer, "the beer that made Milwaukee famous," and all the brands owned by these two brewing companies. Roger's role was critical to these successful acquisitions. To survive, Stroh had to make these moves to increase brewing capacity and expand distribution for Stroh's beer, and Roger and his team made them happen. Stroh had grown from the eleventh-largest brewing company to third, producing twenty-four million barrels of beer annually at its peak yet still behind Anheuser-Busch and Miller. Roger was doing his job. I cannot be the judge of what he did or didn't produce; I was left with the impression that some of the former Stroh executives blame him for the eventual fall of Stroh's beer as a major brand and some credit him for putting up a great fight.

It was our job at AMF, Inc. to supervise communication for these acquisitions as Stroh tried to position itself to compete with the beer industry giants. When the Schlitz acquisition was completed, some media called it the "minnow swallowing the whale," as Schlitz was a publicly owned company and much larger with numerous brands and a wholesaler network in all fifty states. The problem was that Stroh had also accumulated millions of dollars of debt which would later cause huge problems.

The Stroh Team at AMF, Inc.

AMF, Inc. handled all communications for The Stroh Brewery Company, and we grew in the services we provided right along with Stroh itself. This was a tremendous responsibility and opportunity for us all. At one point AMF, Inc. had six staffers working on the Stroh business, and our services were provided in all fifty states. Some of these staffers included Ron Hingst, Bill Sledzik, Barry Bronson, Ted Montgomery (whom we worked with later at JB&A), Mikey Lyons, Lori Roman, Tom Sakley, Tim Johnson, and Lacey Logan. Logan was later hired at Stroh as part of their new internal public relations function. Gerald Lundy worked with us on high level corporate assignments, and Tony Franco would "drop in" from time to time and add his input. Tony told me once that my team and I did 99 percent of the work for Stroh and he did 1 percent, but his 1 percent was as important as our 99. He may have been right...but I doubt it.

The Stroh team at Anthony M. Franco, Inc. also got along well. Like many at Stroh, we worked hard and played hard. At Christmas time Stroh would give us each a twelve-pack of Stroh's beer as a token of appreciation plus four half gallons of the wonderful Stroh's Ice Cream (which came packed in enough dry ice to last twenty-four hours). One year, I handed out all the gifts to the team on a Friday. At the end of the day, one person came in my office with an open Stroh's beer and one for me. Before long, about half the company was in or near my office enjoying our client's beer product. We finished all the beer and were looking for more. Sakley had left early and had forgotten his twelve-pack. That was a huge mistake…you can guess what happened. But we placed all the empty cans back in the case, sealed it, and replaced it near his desk. We all laughed and the memory of this prank brings a smile to me still.

Public Relations Agencies in major cities

To help us keep up with corporate and brand communication across the United States, we researched, interviewed, and added six regional public relations agencies to represent Stroh's beer around the country. They all reported to me. We ended up working with five of the firms in Dallas, Atlanta, Los Angeles, Phoenix, and New York.

But one marketing executive told me that some of the Stroh "new management" often questioned whether they needed a national public relations firm in addition to the Franco firm, which was a Detroit firm—or so they thought. (Some people think all a firm has to do to be national is to be based in New York City—whether or not they are as good as firms outside that locale. This is true for both advertising and public relations firms. This national vs. Detroit perception is something I would fight for years at JB&A when we served numerous clients nationally.) But Anthony M. Franco, Inc.

kept doing a great job for Stroh, and the issue never materialized. Thank you very much.

The Stroh sponsorships grew from state, to regional, to national through major concerts and major sporting activities. The company-sponsored Indy car, Formula One, and NASCAR race teams had a major sponsorship with the National Hockey League, important national singing groups, and bands as part of the "Schlitz Rocks America" campaign.

The Lady Stroh's LPGA Golf Tournament

In the Michigan market, Stroh sponsored the Lady Stroh's, a Ladies Professional Golf Association (LPGA) Golf tournament in 1978 and 1979 at the Dearborn Country Club in Dearborn, Michigan. Both were huge successes for the LPGA, the golfers, and spectators. Attendance records were established for a first year tournament and statewide media coverage was outstanding. At the time some of the stars on the LPGA tour were Sandra Post, Judy Rankin, Jan Stevenson, Laura Baugh, and rookie sensation Nancy Lopez. The LPGA loved our event and wanted a long-term relationship. Sandra Post won the 1978 tournament in a sudden-death playoff and Vicki Fergon won the 1979 tournament just ahead of Judy Rankin.

Again I worked closely with M. John MacLeod, Stroh sales promotion manager, on just about all of these Stroh sponsorships including the LPGA tournaments. We were an excellent team. MacLeod chaired the 1978 Lady Stroh's Open and Peter Remick Stroh chaired the 1979 event. Again, at AMF, Inc., we handled publicity for the sponsorships and ran the press centers for the two tournaments. One of my ideas to help promote the tournament across Michigan and to hopefully lead to attendance at the tournaments was to have amateur golf-qualifying events in key markets in Michigan. The winners would get to play in the pro-am and the LPGA event itself. This worked and the local press also followed their "native daughters" to the Lady Stroh's Open itself. It was great for the event, the golfers and for Stroh's, as press coverage across the state mentioned Stroh's in a very positive way. One of the women I talked to for this book played in the Lady Stroh's in 1978 had nothing but praise for the opportunity as a young amateur to play with the best women golfers in the world. She said that the experience gave her the confidence to choose a career path and get her first job as a sales representative. At least one other young amateur became a professional golfer on the LPGA tour.

Stroh senior management cancelled the sponsorship, saying it did not target the proper audience. I was told by more than one person that the decision was Roger's. I thought that because the event was so successful and attracted male and female, as well as young and old, sports enthusiasts from across the region, that is was a huge success in the home state of Stroh's beer. But I did not have a vote in the decision.

Stroh also participated in or sponsored such nation-wide events as the 1982 World's Fair in Knoxville, Tennessee, and the restoration of the Statue of Liberty in 1984 and '85. AMF, Inc. coordinated public relations activities for all including the Stroh's Run for Liberty to support the statue restoration event in both those years. The Stroh's Run for Liberty was a nation-wide series of running events designed to raise funds for the restoration. Lee Iacocca, then Chairman of Chrysler Corporation, was the national chairman. The Stroh Brewery Company gave Iacocca a check for $3 million for the restoration, one of the largest corporate contributions outside of Chrysler.

The Stroh Brewery Company also established a minority marketing and community relations department headed by Larry Bleach as Community Relations Director. Larry was a star basketball player at the University of Detroit (1933–1936) and its first African American captain. The goal of this department was to reach out to the African American community by promoting Stroh efforts to support African Americans in every way. Obviously Stroh also wanted African Americans to buy Stroh's beer. Former Philadelphia Eagle and Detroit Lion Jim Thrower joined Larry after his playing days ended.

Stroh River Place

By the mid-1970s sales growth serviced by the one Detroit plant had the effect of squeezing out all non-production functions on the landlocked plant site. With the completion of Detroit's Renaissance Center in 1977 Stroh leased space in tower 200 to relocate its growing marketing organization. Shuttles were established to move staff back and forth the approximate one mile from the brewery to the Renaissance Center. In an effort to find a building adequate to house the growing corporate organization, the Parke Davis office building at the foot of Jos. Campau Street became an option. Warner-Lambert, the owner of the building at that time, had moved out and Stroh acquired the 65,000 square foot river front office building and the entire 20-acre site with the encouragement from the Detroit Mayor's office and Warner-Lambert. This was the catalyst for developing the site and to house the nearly 800 person Stroh corporate staff. The company moved into the space in around 1980.

This beautiful, historically designated site is located on the bank of the Detroit River directly across from Canada. The main building was designed by Smith Hinchman Grylls and competed in 1926. The five hundred thousand-square foot, multi-tenant general office and retail building was designed by Albert Kahn and built in two phases in 1929 and 1938. James Steward Polshek Associates were retained to do the master planning and design and construction on the complex in 1984. The site now includes a secure parking structure, 301 residences, and a 108-room hotel. Current Chairman and CEO of the Stroh Companies, John W. Stroh III, said of the property complex,

"Our commitment to Detroit's history and its spectacular riverfront is what prompted us to maintain the architecture of this landmark development." The main building became Stroh headquarters. The site now called Stroh River Place remains a beautiful location and a tribute to the Stroh family and to Peter W. Stroh himself.

In the mid- and late 1980s, Stroh diversified into other beverages, including White Mountain Cooler, a fruit-flavored drink with 5 percent alcohol, and non-alcoholic Sundance sparkling water fruit drinks. Some say they were first into a new category of drink or "New Age Beverage" category. This was a major step forward and would offer Stroh the chance to compete outside the beer industry. Distribution of these new products would not be through their beer wholesalers, which I am sure, did not make them very happy. John Bissell was promoted to Stroh Senior Vice President Special Products and President of Stroh Foods. This separate entity was established to develop and market products other than beer and harkens back to the 1979 study that said Stroh could not survive long-term in the beer business.

Sundance was successful, reaching $100 million in sales at its peak in a very short time, but the parent company needed cash to run its brewing business just to compete. Bissell was given the job to find a buyer for Sundance and therefore, eventually sell himself out of a job. In 1989 Sundance was sold to the US operation of Guinness beer for $100 million, and two years later the product was gone. John Bissell to this day wonders what would have happened if Sundance had continued on, as it was doing very well in the short time it was around.

The Last Year's for the Stroh Family brewing Stroh's beer:

In May of 1989, I departed AMF, Inc. and was no longer involved with Stroh. It was a tough time for me as I loved the Stroh family, the company, and its products, and was close to so many Stroh executives. We had done so much together. The company fought hard to grow and almost did survive. It almost merged with Coors two different times and attempted to purchase G. Heileman Brewing Company, brewers of Heileman's Old Style Beer. It made money contract brewing for Pabst and smaller brewers like Sam Adams and Pete's Wicked Ale. It expanded overseas with some success. Roger Fridholm left and Bill Henry took over as President and later CEO, the first non-Stroh to hold both top positions. In 1996 Henry led the company to finally purchase Heileman. Stroh was later sold to Pabst and the Miller Brewing Company in 1999. Sadly, the Stroh family was out of the beer business in this country for the first time since 1850. Stroh's beer does still exist and can be found on a limited basis. Perhaps if the company had merged with Coors, Stroh's beer as a major brand might have survived, but that did not happen.

CHAPTER 7

THE MEDIA

I have told people working for me throughout my career that if you get to know what the media want, how and when to get it to them, and how to deal with them, you do yourself a great service and that capability cannot be taken away. You make yourself valuable to the media, your client, or employer and most importantly, to yourself as the owner of this important service. Don't get me wrong here. I always tried to position my clients in the most positive way possible. But sometimes the story is negative, but even then, by understanding the media and working with them, you have the chance to get reported the most positive side of the negative issue. For example, if you are laying people off, the layoff positions the company to survive going forward and has the potential to provide jobs and careers for the remaining employees. If you don't work with the media, you may not get the "surviving employee point" in the story about the layoffs.

During my AMF, Inc. years, I got to know media around the country and learned so much about how to work with them and what they needed for a good story. I got to know the Detroit media extremely well and became close, life-long friends with many media people. Stroh had a suite at the Joe Louis Arena, the downtown Detroit sports and entertainment venue. I would host numerous media people in the suite several times each year, usually at Detroit Red Wing hockey games. I went out of my way to get to know them and to learn what they liked and what they didn't like, and that served me well throughout my business career. Many of those Detroit-based media people ended up in key positions from New York to L.A. and in between, including Detroit. This was a huge benefit to me.

One time all my skills were needed. A newspaper reporter over-heard talk about a potential Stroh acquisition while sitting in the lobby at the Stroh HQ. He later interviewed Peter about his original story idea but went back to the office and wrote up the other story. The reporter was not wrong; he was doing his job and did that very well.

He called me later to get some details about the new subject. This new story was a surprise to me. I reported this to Peter, and he said, "John, that story must not run." He said a story might ruin the high-level negotiations they we are conducting which would benefit both Stroh and the city of Detroit, and the story could terminate the deal itself. I tried to explain that you can't just get a story delayed or cancelled, but Peter was adamant it would not run. I called Neal Shine, the publisher of the *Detroit Free Press*, whom I knew well, and I explained the situation. I told him there was no alternative, the story must not run at this time and that Peter was adamant that if it did, the story could impact negotiations that would benefit Stroh and the City of Detroit. I promised that I would make every effort to get the reporter the exclusive when the story was ready for publication. (Note: I did not guarantee the exclusive.)

I waited the two longest hours of my life. Eventually the phone rang; it was Neal Shine. He said, "The story is on hold for now, but we do want the exclusive when it is ready for publication." I called Peter with the news; he expected that result.

In another example, a hot-shot attorney-public relations professional from a New York firm was pontificating in a meeting with top management at Stroh about his media contacts around the country, including Detroit. His firm was working with Stroh on one of the acquisitions, and he was trying to get all the business for the project—including what our assignment was—for his company. He talked about how well he knew the *New York Times* bureau chief stationed in Detroit and that he could "guarantee" a good story about the Stroh purchase. I was sitting next to the vice president we reported to at Stroh. I handed him a note that said, "That person is no longer at the *New York Times*." He had also mispronounced his name, and I told my contact that as well. Plus, I told him no one can guarantee a story on anything. My contact took it from there, and we did not lose any business to that person's firm.

A reporter called once and said, "I understand gays drink Stroh's Beer," sounding like that was a problem. I don't know what he expected me to say, but after a pause I asked, "And what is the problem with that?" After a few seconds, he hung up. There was no story to begin with. There are so many more examples, experiences, and local, regional, and national stories, that it requires another book. Most are good; many are funny. All this experience gained during almost fourteen years was invaluable to my future career. It helped mold me into the professional that I became.

Peter W. Stroh

I grew to love the Stroh family, especially Peter. They were moral, honest, and hard-working—like my parents—and like me, loved the City of Detroit and felt a responsibility to make it a better place. The family was behind many major projects in Detroit over the years at Belle Isle, Hart Plaza, and others, and Peter was on most community boards during his time and received many awards, including the Spirit of Detroit Award and the first *Crain's Detroit Business* Newsmaker of the Year in 1985. He supported the Detroit

Symphony Orchestra, The Detroit Institute of Arts and the Detroit Zoological Institute. He was a great example of supporting one's community and loving one's family. I will always cherish the times I spent with him, and I wish there had been more. When I left AMF, Inc., Peter sent me this note on June 9, 1989:

Dear John;

Many thanks for your thoughtful note regarding your new challenge. We will all miss you here. We have been through a lot together and I would like to express my appreciation for the consistently helpful advice that you gave us during the years that you were with Franco.

All here join me in wishing you the very best.

Signed:
Sincerely, Peter

On a lighter note, once on a business trip together Peter realized he did not have enough cash to get his car out of parking. He asked if he could borrow $10. All I had were three $20s and he would not take $20, he only needed $10. We got change. The next morning a check for $10 was delivered to my office. I wish I had not cashed it.

He was a soft-spoken gentleman who loved the outdoors and was an avid fly caster, bird hunter, and bird watcher. One Stroh executive told me the story that one time Peter called him to come *quickly* to his office. When he arrived the lights in the office were out and Peter whispered, "Come in, close the door quietly." He did, whereupon Peter asked him to join him crawling on hands and knees to the window where a special bird was perched in the tree outside Peter's office.

Peter W. Stroh passed away in 2002 at age 74.

The Stroh Staff

The Stroh staff members were my friends. There were about forty people, mostly men, whom I worked with on a regular basis. Peter W. Stroh, Roger Fridholm, John Bissell, John Hellweg, M. John MacLeod, Patrick J. Fox, Norman Swanson, Tom Schulthorpe, Larry Bleach, Lester Freidinger, James Thrower, Bill Weatherston, George Kuehn, Michael Porter, Chris Lole, Peter Remick Stroh, Bob Ewers, and Mary Dufty are a few I worked closest with and learned from. They worked hard and some, especially the old guard, played hard—but always got the job done.

Many times a large number of Stroh marketing executives would go to lunch at Joe Muer's Restaurant on Gratiot Ave., not far from the old brewery. I know they collectively must have been the best customers Joe Muer's ever had. I attended many of those luncheons and sometimes, dinners. They were great fun. Muer's was a five-star seafood restaurant on Gratiot Ave. near downtown Detroit.

I was close to the marketing team, both the new and old. One morning I was presenting a public relations project to them. The budget was something like $4,000 additional over our existing annual budget. In my concluding remarks, I mentioned that the $4,000 must be about what was spent at Joe Muer's each month by Stroh marketing staff. They looked at each other in agreement and approved the project. I can't remember for sure, but after the meeting we most likely went to lunch at Joe Muer's.

The AMF, Inc.'s efforts on behalf of The Stroh Brewery Company's national expansion were recognized when the publication *Public Relations News* selected our effort as one of the top ten public relations programs for 1985. The program was entitled: "A Many-Faceted Program for Enhancing Recognition of a Company and its Products."

Lessons Learned from working with Stroh are numerous:

- **Respect.**
- **Work hard.**
- **Listen.**
- **Be open to new ideas.**
- **Anything can be done, so do it.**
- **Be responsible and always do your best.**
- **Be honest at all times.**
- **Know the media; you are partners and you need each other.**
- **Challenge yourself to go to the next level.**
- **Your time is not your own...no such thing as a forty-hour week.**
- **Always strive to do your best.**
- **Do not drink too much.**

There is so much more to these critical years. I made life-long friends, learned my profession, and served a great company—The Stroh Brewery Company—and a great family, all while working for one of the top public relations agencies in Detroit and the mid-west. My Stroh experience requires another book.

Important historical dates for The Stroh Brewery Company:

- Began brewing in Germany in 1770s
- Founded in Detroit in 1850
- Built Detroit brewing facility in 1912
- Survived prohibition by producing Stroh's Ice Cream, soft drinks and near beer : 1918–1933
- Purchased Goebel beer in 1964
- Hired Roger Fridholm in late 1970s
- Began national expansion in mid-1970s
- Added Stroh Light as a brand in 1978

- Purchased the Parke Davis facilities in 1979
- Purchased Schaefer Beer in 1981
- Acquired Schlitz beer in a hostile takeover for $17 per share in 1982
- Introduced Signature Beer, the Stroh's super premium beer in 1982
- Added the Special Products Division late 1980s
- Closed its Detroit brewing facility in 1985
- Began selling off its brewing and can plants late 1980s thru mid-1990s
- William Henry named President/CEO in 1991
- Purchased G. Heileman Brewery Co. in 1996
- Sold the SBC to Pabst and Miller in 1999

Some of the brands that were owned by Stroh, many of them acquired through the Schaefer and Schlitz acquisitions and others developed internally:

1. Stroh's Beer
2. Stroh Light
3. Stroh's Draft Light
4. Goebel beer
5. Goebel Light
6. Signature beer
7. Schaefer beer
8. Piels beer
9. Schaefer's Cream Ale
10. Schlitz beer
11. Schlitz Genuine Draft
12. Old Milwaukee beer
13. Old Milwaukee Light beer
14. Old Milwaukee Genuine Draft
15. Schlitz Malt Liquor

16. Old Milwaukee NA
17. Stroh's NA
18. Old Milwaukee Ice
19. Schlitz Ice
20. Schlitz Ice Light
21. Schlitz Light Ice
22. Schaefer Ice
23. Bull Ice
24. Red River Valley Select lager
25. Red River Valley Honey Brown Ale
26. Red River Valley Select Red Lager
27. Old Style
28. Colt 45
29. Special Export
30. Rainier
31. Schmidt's Lone Star
32. Champalle
33. Mickey's
34. White Mountain Cooler
35. Henry Weinhards
36. Sundance

CHAPTER 8

ANTHONY M. "TONY" FRANCO

I learned a lot from Tony Franco too—a lot about business and how to network. What to wear to events, where to sit, what to do, and what not to do. My dad told me that if you learn to walk with the elephants, sooner or later people will think you are an elephant. This is in reference to associating with really important people. No one did that better than Tony Franco. But I also learned how not to treat people from Tony.

Tony was one of the best business and sales persons I ever knew, but he wasn't such a great public relations practitioner—at least I thought that—but he made up for that by hiring the best public relations professionals he could find. But sometimes Tony treated people poorly; he had a—as he called it—"hot Italian temper." Sometimes throughout the office we would all hear him yelling and swearing at an employee like they were idiots. That really hurt me, but not as much as the person being yelled at. Another time, during a closed-door management meeting, several people were late and knocked and entered the room one at a time each interrupting Tony. After about three such interruptions, he said angrily—in a way that sounded real to me—"the next person who walks through the door is fired."

The next person was his friend, senior executive vice president Dick Kelley. We all waited but Tony said nothing.

Tony had built the best public relations company in the region because he hired the best people and public relations professionals—we were the best. Many of us went on to be very successful at running our own public relations firms. Some of these include: Gabe Werba, Robert F. Falls, Lisa Valley-Smith, Jeff Caponigro, Mike Niederquell, Joyce Cusmano, Ron Hingst, and if I may, John Bailey.

Tony was a "mover," though, and associated with all the right business men and women in the community. He accomplished a lot and became chairman of the Detroit Regional Chamber of Commerce which would be one of his most important centers of influence for new business opportunities. But, in my opinion, he never had the kind of prestigious client list that he should have had with the great staff he had and that we would have years later at JB&A. But that is my opinion and debatable.

My best friends during my almost fourteen years at AMF, Inc. were Gerald Lundy and Ron Hingst. Gerald was the best writer and best public relations strategist I ever knew and a beautiful human being. In his career, almost by himself, Gerald won three Silver Anvils—the Oscar of the public relations industry. We started at AMF, Inc. within a few days of each other in 1975. Later I would recommend Gerald for a position at Casey Communications that he accepted. Gerald was inducted into the PRSA-Detroit Hall of Fame in 2001 along with another friend at AMF, Inc., Gabe Werba. Both of these fine gentlemen and public relations professionals have passed away.

Anthony M. Franco, Inc. grew in size and number of employees throughout the 1970s and '80s. I not only served Stroh, but also Domino's Pizza, another of the firm's largest accounts for several years. Domino's Pizza is a national firm that produces and delivers pizza to your home. I started at AMF, Inc. as an assistant account executive and ended up EVP. We added so many people that it was hard to keep up. One time after I had been at the firm only two years or so, Tony promoted a professional to vice president that I knew could not produce like I could. I was so angry I went into my little office and slammed the door so hard that the ceiling tiles blew out. I was standing on my desk replacing the tiles when Tony walked in and asked, "What the heck are you doing?" "Oh, nothing," I said. I was patient and busted my butt and within a year was vice president and never looked back. The person who had been promoted ahead of me flamed out and left the company.

Earlier I mentioned how some people think just because an advertising or public relations firm is located in New York City that it is national and somehow better than a firm located in Detroit. The reality is that each firm should be judged by what it can do for you—the client—and not only by where it is located. When Ron Hingst left AMF, Inc. in 1981, he went to Domino's Pizza as head of public relations. Domino's Pizza was also one of AMF, Inc.'s largest clients and one I headed up. Tom Monaghan, founder and then owner of Domino's pizza, wanted to hire a New York public relations agency because it would be in New York City. Ron knew we were doing a good job for Domino's Pizza and there was no need to hire another firm. But Tom was adamant and Ron had to make this happen. Ron asked me if I knew of any good firms and I recommended one that I knew was a strong firm and Domino's Pizza hired that firm.

As the same time, Mikey Lyons, an outstanding young public relations professional for us working on the Stroh and Domino's Pizza business, announced that she and her husband were returning to their home in New York City, where he had a job waiting. I put Mikey in touch with the same public relations firm, and they hired her. She ended up working on the Domino's Pizza business and would call me once in a while and laughingly tell me they were doing some of the same things for Domino's Pizza that we had done. We laughed, but it really wasn't funny as we had lost the business. I don't know how much more, but Domino's Pizza was paying the New York firm a lot more than they paid us. There is one thing you can be sure of regarding public relations firms located in New York City. They almost always charge more than firms based in Detroit; they have to, as their payment for rent and just about everything else is higher than in Detroit.

At AMF, Inc., I was part of the management team. We met regularly to discuss company issues and to make decisions but...we always did what Tony wanted. There was only one vote on decisions, his. This treatment of many great business and public relations professionals taught me what I would *not* do when I had my own management team...if I ever had one. In the management meetings, we talked about running a profitable company. We talked about profit goals, production, markups, billable hours per employee (professional service hours billed to the client), and for the company. We always did what Tony wanted, but I did learn about those subjects. We never did learn how profitable the company was or how much we were really making. And the rest of the employees knew even less. I made note of this treatment as, again, another example of what I would *not* do.

The treatment of these top professionals not only was frustrating but also turned many of us away from Tony and the company in one way or the other. I just knew I could do a better job if I ever had my own firm.

The Securities and Exchange Commission

The following is a direct quote from the August 27, 1986, *Detroit Free Press*.

"PR EXECUTIVE CITED IN INSIDER TRADING CASE"

"Anthony M. (Tony) Franco, owner of Michigan's largest public relations firm and president of the Public Relations Society of America, was accused of insider trading in a client company's stock and consented to a permanent court order barring him from fraudulent stock-market activity, federal officials said Tuesday."

"The court order settled a civil complaint against Franco by the U.S. Securities and Exchange Commission, which polices stock trading. The order entailed no fine or other penalty, and Franco neither admitted nor denied wrongdoing."

Stories ran in Detroit and Michigan and national news media. Of course, the public relations press covered the story extensively. As I recall several new business prospects decided against working with us and several clients were concerned about continuing to work with us. Because Tony was president of the Public Relations Society of America, the story was on the front page of the *Wall Street Journal* with a sketch of Tony. He resigned the PRSA position. This was really bad PR for a PR guy. The damage to the AMF, Inc. image was done.

Peter Stroh called me to his office. He said, "If it wasn't for the relationship we have with you John, we would terminate our association with AMF, Inc. immediately." He gave us six months like probation. I was flattered and mortified that my company was in trouble with our largest client. We continued working with Stroh for three more years, but it wasn't long before assignments and income began to decline. They terminated the relationship with the firm several months after I left Anthony M. Franco, Inc. in 1989.

Lessons Learned: *You can learn from any situation. Be nice to your employees, it will pay off. Always be honest and do what is right. There is no alternative. Listen and learn from every person and opportunity. Expand your base beyond your local community.*

THE POWER OF OWNERSHIP

Tony Franco sold AMF, Inc. in the late 1990s and left the company. Tony passed away in 2002. Today the firm is called the Franco Public Relations Group and is a strong public relations agency serving a wide variety of clients.

In 1978 I was forty years old and made $35,700. This was behind pace, but I learned so much and was ready for more. I truly believe that my desire for more and to do the best job possible always in any situation, was my way of "owning" the direction of my career but the real "owning" was yet to come. By 1988 I was fifty and making $75,000...still behind but gaining. In all those years I received bonuses ranging from $2,000 to $6,000 as well. I was making $78,000 per year when I left AMF, Inc. to join Casey at $70,000.

John (R) meets Michigan Governor William G. Milliken, along with President of the Michigan Jaycees, Patrick J. Duggan (L), in 1969. Governor Milliken was the first but not the last Michigan governor John would meet. Duggan is now a United States Federal Judge.

This publicity photo staged by John appeared on the front page of the November 5, 1973 *Detroit News*. It promoted the Dodge car and truck involvement for the 1974 Detroit Auto Show. It was John's first "front page" hit for a client.

John and LPGA rookie sensation Nancy Lopez in 1978. Nice jacket John.

"18-Wheels of Love" - 5 trucks driving Stroh's beer from Detroit to begin sales in North Carolina. The name *"18-Wheels of Love"* comes from a song performed by The Serfs, which included my friend Frank Buscemi.

Spring training photo at the Chicago White Sox camp in the mid-1970s. L to R, John, Hall of Fame radio announcer Harry Caray, and Eric Stroh.

Peter Remick Stroh addressing the crowd at the Cincinnati Reds Riverfront Stadium. Stroh's beer sponsored the MVP for each of the Reds Farm Teams. Stroh was presenting the awards.

Brewery Park Site Development

Stroh Brewery Site—1984

Implosion—April 1986

Brewery Park—June 1987

Brewery Park—The Future

Brewery Park Site, home of The Stroh Brewery Company and its first brewing facility. The photo shows the four stages: the original brewing plant, implosion, after the property was cleaned out, and the architect's rendering – later completed - of the new building. 1984–1987.

Stroh's beer hosted the delegations for most of the states that attended the 1980 GOP convention in Detroit. The parties were hosted at the Strohaus, a huge party tent, and tours of the brewery were conducted and delegates got to sample Stroh's beer. At one point, seventeen local television stations from across the country were touring with their delegates and sending footage home. It was great exposure for Stroh's beer, which was attempting to expand nationally. This is most of the team that worked the events. John is the only one wearing a tie.

Stroh's beer sponsored the "Stroh's Run for Liberty" in 1984 and '85, which consisted of running events in many cities across the country. Funds were raised for the restoration of the Statue of Liberty. This photo was used to promote the event. The Stroh Brewery Company contributed $3million in addition to sponsoring the events and drawing national attention to the restoration.

The Stroh Team in 1986. Standing L to R, Barry Bronson and Ted Montgomery; seated L to R, Lori Roman and Mikey Lyons. Each is holding a bottle of the Stroh's super premium beer, Signature. John took the photo.

CHAPTER 9

CASEY COMMUNICATIONS MANAGEMENT/SHANDWICK

The AMF, Inc. and Stroh years paved the way and gave me direction. I was now on a career path and I knew it—that was *the* key. I had built a regional and national network of business and public relations professionals as well as political leaders. I had met with numerous public relations agencies around the country and had worked with six of them. But there came a day in 1989 when I knew it was over at Anthony M. Franco, Inc., and that I had to move on. The Stroh's beer account had basically left the firm by then, and our staff was down to me and one or two occasional support professionals. And Stroh itself was struggling to hang on. We were working with Stroh River Place, the residential, office and apartment complex owned by the family. It was a great account and I was proud of the work we were doing.

For fourteen years I had worked hard and done the best job I could for my clients, including Stroh and my employer AMF, Inc. I had been part of the process at Stroh of growing from two brands in eleven states to many brands in fifty states, a huge experience for me. I had helped AMF, Inc. grow into the largest firm in the region. The question was, "Should I start my own company?" I felt I had the ability, knowledge, and contacts to do so but didn't think I could afford it because of college expenses (Karen and Beth were now at MSU), and frankly, I did not have the confidence that I would succeed. I did not think I was ready for a business ownership but I was taking ownership of my career.

I was sitting in my office pondering my next steps when the phone rang. It was Jack Casey, owner of one of Tony Franco's most bitter rival firms, and very prominent public relations professional. I knew Jack from around town, from the PRSA, and through Jeff Caponigro, who had worked at Franco as a young professional and was in line to be president at Casey, after Jack retired. Jack said he had sold his company, was retiring in a couple years, and needed to bolster senior management staff, and with all my contacts, did I know of anyone who might be interested? What perfect timing. I said, "Yes, me." I joined Casey Communications Management as senior vice president in May 1989 and stayed there until February 1996, when I left to form JB&A. I would then have worked with arguably the three top public relations professionals in the Detroit region (at least from that era) and would see how each worked with their staffs. I did not know how important it would be, but I also got to see how each "removed themselves," or retired, from their companies when the time was right and how much they didn't like each other.

Lessons Learned: *Knowing people is a huge benefit and luck and really good timing is everything, but you must be ready to take advantage of the good luck. Build a network and keep it alive by staying in touch. When you have stopped learning and growing on the job, it is time to make a change.*

I worked with Jack Casey—the man—for about two years before he retired. Before Jack left he gave all employees a significant bonus from the funds from the sale of the firm. This was a wonderful gesture appreciated by all, and I made note for future reference. Jack, in my opinion he was the smartest public relations practitioner I ever knew and the best strategist out of the big three: Beltaire, Franco, and Casey. And his knowledge of politicians and politics was genius. Jack Casey was inducted into the PRSA Detroit Hall of Fame in 1994. I remained with Casey Communications Management for more than six years, and by the end of that time, the company had become Shandwick-Detroit Public Relations. Shandwick was a London-based public relations conglomerate that went around the globe purchasing strong local public relations firms to build a huge international public relations agency. From what I understand, Shandwick had looked at AMF, Inc., too, but decided that management outside of Tony—although good public relations professionals—had not been developed enough as managers of the company. Tony missed a great opportunity and once again, I made note.

Lesson Learned: *Work hard. It pays for your company and its clients and, most importantly, you.*

Traffic Safety Now (TSN)

Jack Casey had built a very strong strategic public relations firm. The most significant account at the firm was Traffic Safety Now (TSN), worth billings of more than seven figures annually to the Casey firm. TSN was a national, non-profit organization of automotive manufacturers and government agencies that pooled money to mount a nationwide public relations campaign to educate the public to the benefits of wearing safety belts.

When the program began in 1984, safety belt usage in cars was about 10 percent nationally. That same year, 44,200 people were killed, and 1.2 million went to emergency rooms. TSN was formed to pass safety belt-use laws in all states—the only effective way to get people to regularly use safety belts. The aim was to reduce the number of deaths of motor vehicle occupants and the severity of injuries, by establishing a nationwide network of grass-roots coalitions leading to hundreds of thousands of volunteers.

Casey Communications had done a fabulous job with the TSN program from the beginning. The company had earned its own Silver Anvil from the Public Relations Society of America for its efforts. Many people worked on the project and had done an excellent job before I arrived at Casey. The credit for this huge success goes to all those Casey employees who worked the project before me. I was very fortunate to begin working on the program in 1989 and became the head of the account in 1990 through to its conclusion in 1992. There was a lot of work yet to do, and this effort took me on numerous trips across the United States to events we had planned to get laws strengthened or passed and to get strong, positive media coverage for the benefits of wearing safety belts. The Chrysler, Ford, and General Motors representatives, the largest contributors to TSN, privately asked me to always do what I thought was the right thing to do. That is what I did then, before, and always.

One of the goals of the last two years of the campaign was to target young drivers, those just learning to drive, and those who had just started driving, with the message that all occupants of a car should wear safety belts all the time. The TSN organization believed that if young drivers began their driving experience always wearing safety belts, it would become a habit, and they always would wear them, and they would also remind others like their parents and other elders to wear the belts. We hired popular professional athletes to speak out to this target audience in support of the effort in their communities and teen television personalities, like Luke Perry and Kellie Martin, two very popular teen stars; he from the hit television show *Beverly Hills 90210* and she from the hit television show *Life Goes On*. They appeared in press interviews and photos and spoke out in support of young people wearing safety belts and encouraging their parents to do the same.

At the conclusion of the TSN campaign, safety belt usage was in the 70+ percent range. This change in American social attitude was called by *Prevention Magazine* in 1992 *"the most significant change in American attitude of the 20th century."* Indeed, an American revolution. Safety belt usage is now at or more than 90 percent in the United States.

A December, 2012, report indicated that traffic deaths were just over 32,000 for that year, down more than 12,000 over the beginning of the campaign and the lowest in decades. This is the result of lots of things, but the safety belt campaign was a major contributor.

Takata

Another important client I worked with while at Casey/Shandwick was Takata, a Japan-based auto supplier that made seat belts and air bags for the auto industry. In 1995 Takata was involved in the largest recall in automotive history to that point. More than 8 million vehicles were to have their Takata-made safety belt buckles replaced or repaired under a voluntary safety recall campaign conducted by the auto manufacturers involved.

The attention to this recall "broke" one morning with television stations at the Takata headquarters in Auburn Hills, Michigan, and quickly spread across the nation and the world. I talked with hundreds of media people from around the world about this crisis. The story took on new life about a week after the original story, when someone in Europe was quoted as saying the Americans were to blame for the belt failures because while eating in their cars they spilled food products into the buckles that caused the damage. This was not true, of course. Many manufacturers were involved, and the important message was that the manufacturers would replace or repair the buckles at no cost to the consumer and that Takata has produced many fine belt buckles before and since and would cooperate 100 percent with the manufacturers.

I worked on this recall issue and the subsequent new product announcements for Takata for several years and that lead them to hire us after JB&A was formed.

Shandwick

Shandwick was an international public relations agency head-quartered in London that went around the world buying strong firms in major cities. I've forgotten how many firms they ended up purchasing, but they spanned the United States and the world.

The owner/CEO of Shandwick was a very formal Brit, who was fond of saying that he trusted the future of his firm and each office to "young public relations professionals." Since I felt young, I didn't get the message that they were not interested in an over-fifty dude with no great education. At that time, I was the number two person at Casey Communications-Detroit, which we were known as. Our President and CEO, Jeff Caponigro, was in his mid-thirties and fit the description of the young public relations leader that the Shandwick CEO wanted.

In my opinion Shandwick did two very stupid things:

1. They ignored the fact that we "older" folks—anyone over forty years of age—had tons of experience, could help lead their various offices, and some were brilliant public relations professionals.
2. In the fall of 1994, they issued an order that in a couple months we were changing the name of Casey Communications Management—the name it had held for many years—to Shandwick-Detroit.

Jeff and I both expressed to management that to drop the Casey name completely with its strong brand recognition in the market-place was not smart—in fact, it was stupid. We said no one knows who or what Shandwick was; in fact, people mispronounced it "sandwich." At the same time, most key decision makers in the region knew the outstanding reputation of Casey Communications Management. I am sure the same was true with the other firms.

We urged them to make the change in annual steps: first, Casey Communications Management — A Shandwick Company; then Shandwick-Detroit—formerly Casey Communications Management; and finally after two years, Shandwick-Detroit.

They dropped the Casey name immediately and gave us no financial or other support to communicate the new name. Management did some other dumb things—in my opinion—like force outsiders on us as business leaders and change all titles to ones that did not fit in our market. I know Jeff did not like becoming managing director instead of president and CEO. Some of the outsiders were to bill at an hourly rate about double what the Michigan market was used to, which we knew would not work. One prominent executive was to bill $450 for his time, well above the $250 or $300 that was an accepted level for our market for a very senior level professional. It became very difficult to get new business.

Jeff left in 1995 to start his own firm, Caponigro Public Relations, leaving me as "acting managing director." I remained "acting" for seven months. I asked numerous times for an explanation and for their plan for me but got little or no response. My wife, Janet—we were married in 1992—asked me, "What part of the writing on the wall can't you understand?" This was a quote that President George W. Bush would later restate. Janet and I began making plans to take ownership of the rest of my career and start JB&A that winter. We decided I would resign in June, after we took a paid vacation in the spring of 1996.

Most new business calls came to me at this time, and in February 1996 we had several new business calls at Shandwick-Detroit. One was an association of small automotive parts manufacturers called the Michigan Flocking Association. Flocking is the fuzzy stuff you most often find in cars in consoles, trunks, and glove boxes. It is also on some wall paper. Their initial project budget was $10,000 for six months to help them get positive auto industry media coverage during the annual Society of Automotive Engineers (SAE) annual extravaganza in downtown Detroit and beyond. This was too small for Shandwick. The "flockers"—as I came to call them—had been told I was the person they should work with. "Sorry," I told the caller. "We can't work with you."

One new business opportunity that was not too small for Shandwick was the North American International Auto Show (NAIAS). At Casey Communications we had two clients participate in the NAIAS. One, Ameritech, was the first non-auto industry client to be involved in the auto show with its Club Ameritech hospitality suite. This was a structure built inside the exhibit hall to provide office and resting space or lounge during the press preview days for visiting executives. The other client to be involved at the NAIAS was R. L. Polk & Co.

I went home that night and told Janet that we had to move up our departure date.

"When are you thinking?" she asked.

"I am going to resign *tomorrow*," I replied.

"*Tomorrow?*" she said.

"Yes, tomorrow. We are missing business opportunities, and my brain is in conflict."

It simply was not ethical for me to be thinking about my inevitable new public relations business while working at another company, even though the old company obviously was not interested in me.

The next morning, February 20, 1996, I was sitting in my office at Shandwick-Detroit waiting for my 11 a.m. meeting to resign with the visiting Shandwick management representative. The phone rang, and I answered. It was Shawn Kahle (she was V.P. communications at a then strong Kmart).

"I've got some media and presentation training for you to do," she said.

We had done training for Kmart before. Media training is preparing executives for media interviews and teaching them how to use their most important messages while answering media questions. We had also done presentation training for Kmart executives. I told her about my decision to leave Shandwick to start my own firm and that I would not be able to do the training and gave her the name of another Shandwick-Detroit executive to call. She was delighted for me, wished me luck, and asked where I would be located. I told her.

I also met with Rod Alberts, whose business at NAIAS I had been courting, to tell him of my departure. He and Shawn Kahle were the first two "outside" people I informed. Rod appreciated the advance notice so he could begin deciding which public relations firm(s) he would recommend to the NAIAS committee that they should consider working with for the 1997 show.

I resigned from Shandwick-Detroit. They had lost their top two executives within eight months and the two people who brought in the most business to the company. They also had a new name to market. They brought in outsiders to run the office. Within a short time, both Caponigro Public Relations and JB&A were larger than the Shandwick-Detroit office. They eventually closed the Shandwick-Detroit office. I always wondered how much money they lost by not listening. On the other hand, it was the best thing for Jeff and me and all our clients. So I guess I should thank Shandwick for pushing me to take ownership of my career and moving it to the next level, ownership of a company.

A few years later, Shandwick returned to Detroit with a completely new firm called Weber Shandwick, and that firm exists in the market today and as far as I know, it is doing well.

Lessons Learned: *Work hard. Network well. Make tough decisions. Trust your instincts. Take a chance. Do not ever eliminate a name that has a wonderful reputation. Listen to people both above and below you on the org chart.*

Jim Meloche

Meloche was the president of French and Rogers Advertising, a midsized advertising firm that did good work. We hired Jim and his firm at Casey to work with Takata on advertising. Jim encouraged me to start my own firm and even provided spare office space and use of office equipment to help me get started. I would have started JB&A without Jim's support, but he made it much easier. My kids were out of college, and my wife had a great job at General Motors with great benefits. In addition to space, Jim invested $10,000 in JB&A stock. After just three years, I bought Jim's stock back for $90,000; that's how much we had grown.

Jim and I had a plan to offer advertising and public relations to new clients and any of Jim's clients that might be interested. Even though this is a good idea, some clients and/or prospects do not understand how they would work with two firms.

CHAPTER 10

JANET LEE BAILEY

We met in October 1989 and were married in November 1992. She was forty-six years old when we met; I was fifty-one. Our meeting was planned by Diane and Ron Hingst. Ron and I were and are friends and worked together at AMF, Inc. on the Stroh business and later at Domino's Pizza. Diane had been a good friend of Janet's for many years; they refer to each other as sisters. Ron and Diane had a chili party at their home attended by numerous couples and Janet and me. I was late in arriving and Janet almost left. Thank God she didn't. It was chemistry at first sight. We began dating right away, and our first formal date was to the North American International Auto Show. (The auto show keeps coming up. It must be in my future.)

She is my rock. She is my sweetie, my honey. She is my partner. She is the one who keeps me moving in the right direction. She puts up with a lot. (I can be difficult, you know.) Janet has listened to so many struggles at JB&A and has always been there with clear, open, and honest input. She deserves nothing but the best in life, and I know I fall short. She is the sweetest and kindest person ever. She has provided for her mother without complaint for more than thirty years. And she'd do it for another thirty with no hesitation. Never underestimate her. There were only a couple women ahead of her as executive administrative assistant at one of the world's largest corporations. She has tremendous ability and a great memory and sees things clearly and acts quickly. I could not have accomplished as much as I have without Janet Lee. She is my best friend. I love her.

Every Friday night we would go on a dinner-date. Whoever had the worst week would vent while the other listened. When it was my turn to vent, she would often say, "Why don't you do this or that..." and her input always helped me see the situation from another perspective and helped me to make a better decision.

We all need someone to keep us balanced. To share ideas with and to understand what we are trying to accomplish. Janet was the one who was my sounding board on just about every decision from the day I met her in fall 1989 through today.

The fact that she had a great job at General Motors with benefits gave me a safety net and the opportunity to let JB&A become what it could without the pressure of getting those things, at least at the beginning.

While we were at the 1990 NAIAS, one of the features of the Club Ameritech Hospitality Suite was a secure coat check. That is huge, especially on the Charity Preview night. This is the night where 12,000 to 15,000 people dress up in formal wear and at that time paid $400 a person to attend. All the money raised goes to Detroit-area children's charities and has been as high as $7 million one year. It is "*the*" place to be if you are interested in the auto business as you see obviously hundreds of new cars, but most importantly, the people who work in the industry and their spouses. We checked Janet's fur coat, as did other guests of Ameritech, including many celebrities and dignitaries. In fact, singer Aretha Franklin arrived at the same time we did but kept her coat on.

Later that evening two female models walked into the coat check room as bold as could be and walked out with coats that were not their own...one was Janet's and other was owned by the wife of a high-ranking officer at General Motors. We were in good company, but it was no fun having Janet's coat stolen. So instead of attending one of the many afterglow parties, we spent the rest of that evening in the Detroit Police mini-station inside Cobo Hall making the police report.

Three good things happened from that negative situation: 1. Ameritech reimbursed Janet the insurance value of her coat; 2. the General Motor's officer's wife got her coat back, and 3. we got to know Rod Alberts, the NAIAS executive director, even better.

Lessons Learned: *Go to friends' chili parties. Good things can come from bad situations. (I think I've said this before.)*

CHAPTER 11

THE FORMATION OF A NEW
BUSINESS, 1995–1996

Over the 1995 Christmas/New Years' holidays, Janet and I talked about the business, John Bailey & Associates (JB&A) Public Relations. We selected that name because after over thirty years in business in the Detroit area, I had a strong reputation in the business community, the media, and within the public relations industry. Therefore, we thought that name would attract companies to consider doing business with us.

Lesson Learned: *Listen to your spouse. Your spouse is your partner in so many ways.*

At first Janet and I thought if I started the business that I could do OK, get a couple accounts, and make a few bucks until I retired. I thought maybe I'd have an associate or two and wasn't thinking about all those things I might do differently in my own business, the things I thought of during my Anthony M. Franco, Inc. years. The timing was right, as the economy was strong and Janet had a great job at General Motors. But wow, were we wrong. Even though some people thought I was too old, JB&A took off.

I had always thought about starting my own company and all those things I would do differently from past bosses. I also had heard that a person would love being an owner with the freedom to do what she/he wanted, and more money could be made as an owner than being an employee. I honestly wasn't thinking about making a lot of money, just enough. This was my opportunity; I was ready to make the move toward business ownership.

I left Shandwick-Detroit and opened JB&A in an office at the French and Rogers ad agency, thanks again to Jim Meloche. I had no clients and no employees and, of course, no income. I knew I needed an office, not an office at home, because at my age and level of accomplishment, I hoped to be meeting with senior level officers of prospects and clients. So a nice suite in upscale Troy, Michigan, was it.

During the holidays I had written a mission and vision statement and a business plan. I made projections for my first year, March through December, and had lists of strengths and weaknesses. I had a three-tiered list of prospects. And, from my mom, I knew I would always to do what was right.

I had a lot of experience from working with successful business people from my career of more than thirty years, and my firm would be built from that experience. So I borrowed what I thought was the best—and eliminated what I thought was the worst—from John Richard Hurley, Bev Beltaire, Tony Franco, and Jack Casey, and many others, including clients, elected officials, and the media. My Jaycee experience helped as did my community involvement. And I knew I would stick to these principles.

We worked out all the legal papers, and Janet and I each put $10,000 into the JB&A bank account, as did Jim Meloche. We each owned one-third stock in the company, and that $30,000 became our line-of-credit for our first several months' use. I was now the owner of my career and a company and I established a code of guiding principles based on my past experiences and what I had learned were either the right things do or what I had learned were the wrong things to do. I also believed that if you treated your associates well that this would create the best working condition that would lead to the best work. Would this work? We would find out over the next fourteen years.

But I knew several things for sure. I had no formal education on managing a company and on managing people, if we would be so fortunate to have to hire some. If the company was to succeed, I had to learn a lot and fast. I read any book that might give me a better understanding of what I was doing. I read the *One Minute Manager* series by Kenneth K. Blanchard and books by James C. Collins including *Good to Great*, *Built to Last*, *The Last Best*, and *Beyond Positive Thinking*. There were many more over the years, including the books by Jack Welch, *Winning* and *Straight from the Gut*, and *Execution* by Lawrence Bossidy. Plus many specific subject books on crisis management, media and presentation training.

Another thing I knew was that many times, public relations professionals do great public relations for their company or agency and get promoted and have people reporting to them. As often as not, these new managers do *not* know how to manage people. I had learned what people did not like as an employee, so I tried to understand more about what they did like, *or,* how they wanted to be treated. I also knew that you can get more done if a person is managed well and *wants* to do a job because that person's role is understood. This would become the cornerstone of my company. My old theory of any two can get more done than any one became clear as well. This was to encourage everyone to own their job at JB&A. I always told our associates that they were the president of what they do so do the best you can at all times.

I thought that if I could have started a company at the same time as Tony Franco that I could build at least as strong a firm because the power of the people would be on my side. Note I did not say largest, although that might have happened as well. We will never know, but we did have tremendous success in the more than fourteen years of JB&A, and the Franco firm in its many years was very successful. No one knows what we could have accomplished if JB&A had remained in business for twenty-five years or more.

One time during the JB&A years, an old-time media person called me "the new Tony Franco," saying it as a compliment. I took it as a compliment but went out and bought a new book.

The books that I based so much of my management on were the Steven F. Covey series, especially 7 *Habits of Highly Effective People*. These became the style with which I managed and encouraged others to manage during the JB&A years. I bought the books for many of our key people to help them learn how to manage so that we would all be doing the same things while managing ourselves and others. It helped that Mike DeVilling, after he joined us, also believed in Covey and his 7 habits.

John Bailey & Associates Inc.
Public Relations

JB&A Logo

CHAPTER 12

JOHN BAILEY & ASSOCIATES
THE EARLY YEARS, 1996–1998

We got out the press releases and announcements of the new JB&A to appear or run the last week in February 1996. The first day of JB&A was March 1, 1996. I knew my contacts and relationships would be the key to my early success, but I way underestimated their importance.

The phone began ringing from day one. We were off and running. In those early days, whenever I did not have something specific to do, I would contact people on my prospect lists by email or phone. Looking back I would guess I personally reached more than 250 people with emails and/or telephone calls that first month. (This was before Facebook, Twitter, LinkedIn, and other forms of social media.) Newspaper articles appeared announcing the formation of JB&A that supported my personal efforts. I reminded everyone that I was now in business, and if they knew anyone who might need public relations assistance, to give them my name. I would also remind *them* that if ever they needed help, I was there. The point is; I asked for business, I didn't assume they knew I wanted business.

I made that same kind of effort every time I had some open time until I no longer had open time. I was relentless in reaching out to people to remind them that I and we were in business.

Lessons Learned: *Always do a good job—it builds your reputation. Network well and keep your network alive by connecting with them regularly. Ask your contacts for business.*

It was amazing...at the beginning of that month, I did not know what would happen, but I projected $5,000. We hit our target, and that was when I realized that setting realistic goals is essential for every person and business, whether monthly or quarterly, and certainly annually. I also knew that this was just the beginning of something very special.

One of my calls was Shawn Kahle from Kmart. She said, "I have media and presentation training for you. When can you start and would you like us to pay in advance?" I was overwhelmed and thanked Shawn profusely and did the training over the following weeks.

One call came from a Shandwick client who asked when my non-compete agreement was up. I said in one year. She said, thank you, good luck, and hung up. One year later she called and gave us their business. This was Kelly Services, which became our largest client for several years.

The Michigan Flocking Association key executive called and said they wanted to work with me and that the budget was now $20,000 for nine months. This budget was up $10,000 from their first budget estimate. This was awesome news to me.

Then my friend Paula Blanchard (now Stone), who had her own public relations firm, called and said that a major Detroit-area ad agency would like to media train many of its key executives and would I partner with her?

Pricewaterhouse called and gave us their business. This was before they added Coopers.

A friend at the Detroit Convention Bureau called and asked if I would help them establish and write their Crisis Plan—for a fee.

We were growing so fast that I had to add my first associates. Our first was Joanna Lasso, a recent graduate from Kent State University who was recommended by Bill Sledzik, who had worked with me on the Stroh account. Bill was teaching at Kent State and is now associate professor there. Joanna did everything from answering the phone to writing press releases and contacting the media.

We then hired Frank Buscemi, a few months out of Grand Valley State University, as a public relations generalist and writer. Soon after, we hired Curt McAllister who was working for another small public relations firm located in downtown Detroit. We needed Curt to help work on some automotive business we had won. Curt told me that he did not know the automotive media. I told Curt that they are all in one place covering the same stories; you will get to know them well and fast. Curt became—in my estimation—the best automotive media relations person in the industry. He was also the heart and soul of JB&A from the day he walked in the door, and is now head of Toyota public relations in Detroit. Frank also became a very highly successful automotive media relations professional and now heads marketing and public relations for TI Automotive a major auto supplier. Joanna is living with her family, including her husband and three daughters, in Chicago.

I remember the major decision I made when I hired Joe St. Henry, my first senior-level public relations practitioner. Our monthly income at that time was around $40,000. I knew I would have to pay Joe at least $35,000 plus benefits. It was a huge decision and one which I labored over for weeks, losing sleep and worrying. I hired Joe. In his first month, he billed more hours to clients for work done than his salary; we were profitable on his efforts from day one.

In the early years, when we were invited to pitch for public relations business, we would finish in third place behind two other firms. After we began adding professionals with expertise in specific areas of our service and our team of professionals gained more experience themselves, we moved into finishing second, and then finally, we began winning business. It took time and patience for us to become a firm that could win any account, but we would not give up and it happened. At one point we were winning three times out of four, even four times out of five pitches. It was sometimes hectic and led to us adding more associates along the way.

In those days we often presented against Ray Eisbrenner's firm and another great public relations professional, James Bianchi and his firm, especially in the automotive space. Even though we were competitors, we liked and respected each other. Often we would ask the prospect at the end of our presentation, "Which firms are you meeting with?" They'd say Eisbrenner and Bianchi. We'd say, "They are great firms. We'd prefer you to select us, but you can't go wrong selecting any of us." As often as not, the prospect would say, "That is what they said about you too." We all wanted to win of course, but we liked each other and were and remain friends...way unlike the days of Beltaire, Franco, and Casey.

JB&A reached more than $300,000 net sales March through December 1996 and $500,000 in the full 1997 calendar year, both over projections. Our clients included companies in the automotive, healthcare, retail, and financial industries. I had set my salary at $6,000 per month or $72,000 per year for '96 and '97, but I could not pay myself every month. While doing the JB&A taxes in early 1998, Rob Dutkiewicz, our CPA, said, "You owe yourself $30,000 and you have the money, so you can pay yourself now." I was thrilled and went home with a nice check that day. In 1998, we billed over $1 million and had hired several more professionals to support our clients. We reached or exceeded all financial goals in every year until 2008.

Personally, I turned 60 in 1998 and earned $124,000, plus bonus and I owned a significant company that was growing rapidly, and the economy was good.

Lesson Learned: *Do not give up, try harder. Keep digging. Good things will happen.*

CHAPTER 13

THE JB&A GUIDING PRINCIPLES 1996

Here's where you can really learn what it takes to build your career and/or start your own company. These are principles that we followed, and they are not just words. If you ask any of our former associates, they will tell you that we did follow them or tried our best to do so. Some outsiders might say this is BS, but not to me and our associates. They were derived from my experience, listening, my reading, the 7 *Habits of Highly Successful People*, and were just plain "the right things to do."

- <u>Be good to your associates.</u>

  We always tried to offer the best benefits that we could. From days off, to salaries, to vacation days, to hours, to flex-time, we always made decisions "with the associate(s) in mind." I know it cost us money in profits to do this, but it is what we wanted.

We had a goal of "no office hours," just "do your work." If an associate had to take time off for whatever reason, closing on a home, picking up the kids, going to the doctor, etc., we said, do it and let us know when you will be in. We knew that responsible professionals would do their work…and they did, often working well over the standard forty hours.

- <u>Be open and honest with associates sharing all financial details.</u>

  We met regularly and reviewed our financial goals, gross and net sales, profits, and more. We sought their understanding and therefore, appreciation, of their role in the company. The only numbers we did not share were personal incomes.

- <u>Allow associates to achieve the most they can at the firm.</u>

  Don't over-manage. Let people know they are in charge of themselves and can take their job as far as they want to.

  The intent is to have each person know they are the president of what they do. This gives them buy-in and helps keep them thinking about what they can do better. "What would you do?" would be my question to anyone who came to me with a problem. It worked for most people most of the time.

- <u>All ideas are welcome</u>

  If someone came to me and said, "I want to paint the White House (in Washington, DC) purple," my question would be, "Tell me more…what is your thinking?" Positive receptivity to new ideas and thinking encourages people to do just that. Many things we did at JB&A came from this kind of thinking. In fact, our Lansing office was the result of one associate,

Andy Hetzel, presenting his new idea…more on the Lansing office later.

- <u>Any two of us is better than any one of us.</u>

This goes back to my bully story. But a more specific business example is this situation…we were in a creative session with the entire company, about twelve people. We exhausted all ideas for a client special event. We were drained and did not have a really good idea. We were about to end the meeting when we asked for "one more idea." I looked at the youngest, newest associate who hadn't said anything during the meeting. She almost reluctantly gave her idea. It was brilliant. We used it in the presentation to the client and took that person along.

- <u>No one takes credit for successes.</u>

It is a team effort; we will be a "we" firm. We replaced "I" with "*we*" in all letters, memos, and proposals.

- <u>Honesty is the only policy.</u>

There will be zero tolerance on this point. All you have to do is look at the news every day to see examples of companies and/or people who have not done the right thing. For the most part, they are ruined when caught.

- <u>We will support and adhere to the PRSA code of ethics and standards.</u>

The PRSA has a strong code for ethics; we followed it. I carried a copy of the code with me to demonstrate our commitment. For example, some PR firms would work with competing companies or on competing issues. The PRSA Code said no; we never did.

- <u>We will be an equal opportunity employer.</u>

This was automatic and we were.

- <u>We will manage the JB&A finances well.</u>

I learned that if finances are in shape, you will serve your clients better. We were in the top 5 percent of PR firms in the country in getting our monthly invoices out, usually by the fifth of each month. And we paid our bills on time, sometimes even before being paid by the client. We also did not buy things until we had the money it in our budget.

- <u>We will network well and keep our network strong and active.</u>

When I started JB&A, I knew my network would be important, but I had no idea how important. I remained active in organizations meeting people, keeping up with people, and always doing a good job to assist the organization and show that I was a person who always did a good job. We always encouraged our associates to do the same.

- <u>We will serve the public relations community, and that community will be our strongest center of influence.</u>

I became active in the PRSA in the late 1960s. After JB&A was formed, we increased that involvement and became a major supporter and sponsor, and associates joined PRSA and other professional organizations too. From that foundation, we built our reputation as one of the leading firms in the region.

- <u>We will serve the Detroit and Michigan regions and will become a national public relations firm based in Michigan.</u>

That was our goal day one and we did it.

- <u>We were committed to serving our clients to the best of our ability at all times.</u>

By helping our clients accomplish their goals, we achieved ours.

- <u>We will be on the "following edge" of technology.</u>

We could not afford to be the first into new technology because of our small size. We believed that by remaining aware of the latest technology and by observing how the first users achieved success or not, we followed very soon thereafter.

- <u>We will be flexible with our employees allowing them time to do what they need to do in their personal lives while becoming the best possible public relations professional they can.</u>

Our goal was always to de-emphasize specific hours and allow flexibility in work schedules

- <u>We will partner with the news media, both general and trade, to help them get the best stories at all times on or about our clients.</u>

This is a subtle point that some public relations practitioners cannot understand. No matter what the story was: totally positive, totally negative, or somewhere in between, we believed if you work with the reporting media as partners you will maximize your potential to get the best possible story.

- <u>We will always look for ways to grow as a company and as professionals.</u>

- <u>Always look and act bigger than we are as a company.</u>

We did this by working with freelance professionals, by adding interns at various times of the year, by adding the latest professional services, and by networking with other public relations agencies around the country and the world.

Our motto was: Your Reputation is Our Business.

Client Service—Clean Those Ash Trays

We also knew that providing our clients with the best and most efficient service would be the key to keeping them and growing them. And a satisfied client would be a great reference when seeking new business. I knew from past experiences that providing outstanding client service is *the most important aspect of a client/agency relationship*, and this outstanding service takes care of everything else, including profit.

One problem with this is what the client expects from us, or what we called "client expectation." It was up to us to understand what our clients wanted and to explain what our services could do to help them attain their goals. It was and is critical that any and all clients understand what public relations and JB&A could and could not do.

It you reach this understanding, you will most likely have a satisfied client. When we could not get them to understand for any reason, we were in trouble with that client.

But sometimes it is what they see *first* that is important.

Early in my life and career, while we lived in Farmington Hills—in the 1970s, my brother-in-law, Dave Cushing, and I started a janitorial business to earn extra money. We built a strong business and cleaned offices, auto dealerships, model homes, and manufacturing company offices in the evenings. We learned that we could do everything just right, that is, empty all trash containers, vacuum, sweep, wash the floors, and dust everything. But if the ash trays were not cleaned, the customer was not happy. We learned fast to always empty and clean the ash trays...that was what they saw first and always remembered.

This applied to my public relations career too. We always attempted to do what our customers wanted to see first. Sometimes that carried the day while we were making everything else work. If they want to see a positive story in print, forget everything and get them that positive story. Then work on strategy and long-term goals. This is essential to your success in public relations and all business.

This point was something that Mike DeVilling, as the number two guy at JB&A for eight years, expressed to all our associates. He loved this example of the ash trays and uses it to this day at his own public relations firm. A more current way to consider this concept is if you are washing a car make sure the dash board and windows are clean.

By the way, Dave and I built the janitorial company and were one or two accounts away from making the decision to do janitorial full time. We were bidding for the Farmington School District business and might have gotten that business, but we decided to focus on our other careers. We learned we had one advantage over all our competition...we were dependable (and always cleaned the ash trays).

Our other brother-in-law Tony Stines was our best employee as he worked his way through dental school. After two years we sold the business for $3,000, and that was a lot of money.

Lessons Learned: *Manage your client's expectations; always do what they see first and/or want you to do first; always be the company your clients can depend on to deliver.*

CHAPTER 14

JB&A: THE RAPID GROWTH YEARS
1998–2007

The greatest accomplishment of JB&A was the tremendous staff we built. They are great young professionals (not so young anymore) who are growing and challenging themselves every day. And this staff served a truly blue chip list of Michigan-based clients.

Early on I had a policy for hiring that worked. As we grew, we had to change it slightly. Whenever we went away from that policy, we had the potential to add someone who did not fit in. We always hired people that I knew, knew of, knew their work, or knew their boss, or someone who worked closely with them. We were hiring young professionals—people in their twenties for the most part—and that changed as we grew and began adding people with more experience. This also helped us know a little about a person's character and background. We were not as interested in grades in college as we were in whether the person was a self-starter and was motivated to always do the best. Don't get me wrong, we did have several folks who had outstanding records in college.

We also had two or three JB&A associates interview the job candidates, those people the job candidate would work with. I thought this did four things that helped us:

1. We could check for chemistry with the people the potential hire would work with.
2. Their education and experience could be evaluated by the people who had similar recent experiences.
3. We could give our young professionals experience they had never had.
4. We showed our associates that we had confidence in them and gave them a sense of responsibility.

Because of this hiring process, we did an excellent job of hiring in the early years and really throughout our history and staff turnover was very low. It wasn't until later when we began adding people with more experience and who were a few years older that we added a few who did not fit our culture and work ethic. Most of those were good people and professionals; they just did not fit at JB&A.

We also hired and worked with interns throughout our history. We almost always had one to three interns on staff at any given time. This was one way of getting work done and looking bigger than we were. This kept our cost down too, as interns can do entry-level work saving the time of our more senior workers for more involved work. Our policy was to hire recent college graduates as interns for a six-month internship which we could extend if we had work and we chose to do so. Sometimes, especially at auto show time, we would hire people who were still in college; this was also true in our Lansing office, as 40,000 students are just down the road in Michigan State University. Again, JB&A staffers would maintain a file of resumes of young professionals and when interns were needed, we would begin the hiring process.

We found some great young professional talent through the intern program. At one point, we had five former interns on staff as full time professionals whom we hired after their internships expired. Even if an intern was not hired, she/he had a great "notch" on their resume for future job interviews and a great reference from one of the leading public relations firms in the region.

People often ask about the process of firing someone. I learned a long time ago that most people are *really good people.* They just don't fit their current job. So, by firing them, you give them the chance to find out what job they should be in. Numerous times when I fired someone, that person ended up in another job that better fit them or went back to school and learned a completely new profession. As harsh as it sounds, the firing was a new start. Plus, if someone does not fit in to your company, everyone knows it, most likely even that person. So to have the best team of professionals (to clean those ash trays for clients), you need to move quickly and replace that person with someone who fits. I learned that if you keep talking about someone over time who you think "might not be fitting in," she or he is not, so move. A business advisor of mine once said, "Hire slow and fire fast." This is good strategy.

Was JB&A ever fired? Yes. With many more than one hundred organizations as clients over the years, it was impossible not to make a mistake, or not do the job that a client wants or some other event that leads to a termination. But our firings were very few and certainly were in the minority. Most clients were very happy with our service to them and what we charged them. In my past experience, I was used to clients challenging a bill or being unhappy with a bill. We rarely experienced that at JB&A. We billed for what we did and not any more. Our clients were seldom if ever surprised by our bills to them. I always thought, "What would I expect to be billed for this same service." If it was too high, we told the client up front and they approved the expenditure in advance, or we didn't proceed.

Another very important method of keeping costs down while having really strong professionals on staff for client service was to work with freelance professionals. In the early years, we worked with several outstanding public relations professionals like Pat Adanti-Joy and retained their services either on a project basis or part-time basis. Again, not only did we have their input, but also JB&A looked larger as well. We were very fortunate to add the services of one of these outstanding professionals—Gayle Joseph—to our full-time staff. Gayle was with us full-time for over four years, left, returned, and is now managing director and partner of Lambert-Edward Public Relations, Investor Relations in Detroit.

Before leaving the topic of hiring, it is very important to *do background checks on new hires*. You never know what you might find out about a person. One time we hired an office manager who came highly recommended. We did not check the background. Over the next eight weeks, the person embezzled more than $30,000 from us at a time when that was a critical amount of money to us. If we had lost any more funds, we might not have survived. It was at least half of our profit that year. We had business insurance and got $10,000 back, leaving a loss of more than $20,000. We were fortunate to find out before it got any worse, so please learn from my bad experience. The culprit did go to jail for this crime. A background check would have suggested we not hire this person.

In later years, we retained a personnel company to do all our hiring and screening and maintaining personnel records. They also updated our company policy manual which I had drafted as soon as we began hiring associates.

Today there are firms that handle your accounting and books, phone answering, personnel issues, and even legal issues. It is a great way to save money versus hiring full-time associates.

New York Affiliation

We affiliated JB&A with Ruder Finn, New York, and its sister agency, RFBender Public Relations. Together with Ruder Finn and/or RFBender, we presented to several clients over the years and won a few, but this did not catch on like any of us hoped it would. But it did make JB&A bigger and gave Ruder Finn and RFBender major offices in Michigan with knowledge of the automotive industry. I would absolutely do this again. One major client win would make this affiliation a huge success, not just the moderate success it was.

We even reached out globally to agencies in other cities of the world, especially in Europe and China, to attempt affiliations. We would review them just like I reviewed the agencies we worked with while working with Stroh. We checked their client list and web sites and anything else we could, to learn about these agencies. With these agencies we could offer public relations services to our global clients such as R. L. Polk & Co. and NAIAS in other cities around the world. Like our New York affiliation, this worked to some degree, and yes, I absolutely would do this again.

There are organizations or networks of public relations firms too that one could evaluate joining.

Rapid Growth

During these years we grew from $1 million net sales in 1998 to $3.3 million net sales and close to $5 million gross in 2007. We had in the range of twenty to thirty-two associates and added the Lansing office, which was profitable from its first year. Our profits were in the 5 to 12 percent range, which was lower than comparable firms around the country as we always made decisions with the associates in mind. Some public relations firms make in the 20 to 30 percent range.

This profit level was a conscious decision on my part and one which all new business owners need to consider. What is your annual profit target and how do you get it and how do you keep it? We moved from 1,000 square feet to 2,000 square feet in our first office on New King Street in Troy. We then moved to the Top of Troy Building and 5,000 square feet to eventually more than 8,800 square feet, on the eleventh floor of the thirty-five-story building which had become PNC Building. It was a great location on the freeway and was a twenty-minute drive to downtown Detroit. We were working with McCann Erickson, a major national advertising agency, on some of their client public relations work. Also, we were working with Buick Motor Division which was also a McCann client. McCann Erickson had the extra space in the Top of Troy building and sublet it to us for their lease rate which was far better than the going rate at that time in 1998.

Speaking of McCann Erickson, another of their other major clients at that time was GMC Truck division of General Motors. McCann was terminated by GMC. The head of the Detroit office was stunned and asked me what I thought they should do. I said, first of all, run a full page ad in the *Automotive News*—to me the most important publication covering the auto industry—thanking GMC for many years of a great relationship and wishing them the best.

He asked why in the world would we do that? I said for two reasons:

1. It shows you are a good sport and you do wish them the best, and
2. GM is huge; they may still give you some new work and who knows if the new company can do the job they promised? Other prospective clients will be impressed as well.

McCann did run that ad and eventually did get a significant new account assignment from General Motors.

Lesson Learned: *Never, I mean never, burn a bridge. Times and people change and things do come around. Just walk away.*

JB&A – A Top 100 Public Relations Firm

JB&A was ranked nationally as one of the top one hundred largest privately owned public relations firms, and our work in the auto industry made us one of the largest public relations firms serving that industry in the country. I always believed that at our peak, we had more automotive clients than any firm in the country. Not in budget but in number of accounts. Our health care industry practice was also nationally ranked and very strong.

We set up the company management with heads of area groups; for example: health care, automotive, retail, technology, and the Lansing office including public affairs. Eventually, the heads of each of these categories became vice presidents of JB&A.

These individuals were part of the management team, along with Beverly Mattinson, our controller, and me. We literally made all decisions about running the company. I emphasize the "we" rather than "I" or "me." This is also a decision business owners must make. Will you dictate how your business is run or will you listen to others? If you haven't noticed by now, I always listen first before making any decision or recommendation. The management team met once or twice a month, but often more frequently and in the very early morning before the phones began to ring "off the hook."

We tried to keep up with what were the going salaries and billing rates at firms like ours not only in Michigan but around the United States. We paid our associates at or slightly above what others were paying. Those were our goals at least. And not once did a man make more money than a woman in similar positions at JB&A. We also had a great advanced degree tuition refund program which several people took advantage of.

My role as visionary for the company was to guide or direct the management team and to always keep looking for ways to do things better to bring to the team. I also remained in constant touch with the heads of our key clients to be aware of what they were thinking about our service to them. Not only did I monitor our work, but also the professionals who worked on those accounts. This way I was able to catch most problems or potential problems before they became an issue. I always kept our client service as my number one goal.

The management team structure did several things:

- It gave members the opportunity to learn how to run a public relations firm.
- It gave me an opportunity to communicate on a regular basis my vision for JB&A.
- It gave us all opportunity to follow or make decisions based on our guiding principles.
- It served as a learning opportunity for everyone.
- It helped me determine which of those present might potentially replace me as the CEO.
- It kept us aware of what everyone was doing within the company.

Another thing we did was to hold regular full staff meetings in addition to the management meetings. Account teams would report on their significant activities. This was a great way to see where or if others could offer ideas or assistance, and it served to keep me and the management team informed of what was going on throughout the company. Our cafeteria also offered similar opportunities as many folks ate lunch in and talked informally about what they were doing or their boyfriends, husbands, girlfriends, wives, etc. These were fun and educational.

One professional service we were all very proud of was what we called "media breakfasts." We would invite an important journalist to speak to key clients and prospects several times a year. This was a great way for *us* to meet newcomers to town or to learn about a new assignment that a journalist had. We'd invite forty to fifty people to a 8:30 a.m. standup breakfast where we'd all meet the speaker and then have the media person talk for fifteen minutes followed by a fifteen-to twenty-minute Q&A. People were on their way by 9:45 or 10 a.m. It was fun and inexpensive. It impressed the heck out of our clients and prospects and helped us keep up with current events and people in the media. I called it a win, win, win.

Before I go on about JB&A, I'd like to comment on the economy. The economy, especially in a region like Detroit, but also in the nation will have a direct impact on the opportunities that present themselves to you or any new business. In good times there are more opportunities and in bad times, not as many. We were fortunate to have strong economic times during our first twelve years of operation and this helped. But I believe there is no bad time to start a business. You must always keep cost under control, in good times and in bad, but it can be done in both situations. In bad times you might not grow as fast, but you can survive and position yourself well to thrive in the future. I will talk more on the bad times when I discuss the 2008 recession.

Remaining Committed to Who and What You Are as a Company

In thirty years of public relations agency work, I can't remember a client fired until we fired several at JB&A. We knew who we were and the kind of people and companies we wanted to work with, and we would not waiver from that commitment and those ideals. For three consecutive years, we lost our largest client this way and yet still grew year over year.

On two of these occasions, a male employee at our largest client of that year was making frequent inappropriate comments to the female JB&A client contact. After numerous cautions and warnings, we terminated one client. On another occasion we reported the offending person to his female boss. She responded saying all the right words, but two weeks later *we* were terminated. In both cases we thought: good riddance.

Another time, client management asked us to do things that were not ethical. We explained our position, but they kept up their request; we politely terminated them. They were shocked.

Still another time we were working with a client that had a decent annual public relations budget and had the potential of becoming a strong account at JB&A. However, public relations and our efforts were not understood as much as they should have been. We struggled every month to help them understand what we were and could do for them and their goals. Then one day I got a call and they wanted our assistance announcing their new president a Roger Fridholm, the former president at The Stroh Brewery Company. We helped them with the announcement, but I decided (I did on this one) that an already difficult client would most likely become even more difficult; so, we politely resigned their business but remained with them until they decided what they wanted to do.

We also turned down new business that was either unethical based on the PRSA Code of Ethics or that did not fit who we were. We never did work on competing issues or with competing clients. And yet we knew public relations firms that did both.

When making such tough decisions, the JB&A management team and I would always worry about the financial implications to our company. We were potentially talking jobs at JB&A. Those times always reminded me of something Tony Franco said to me, "No matter how much you care, you have no idea what it is like sit in my chair (as owner/CEO) and make payroll and pay the bills every month." At those, and many other, times I did know what it was like. But in every case, we were able to overcome the financial loss and continued to grow. The income was not the most important thing to us, respecting ourselves and what we stood for was.

These are really a very few client situations, like 1 percent. For the most part, our clients were, and are, great people providing great products or services to their markets.

The JB&A Lansing Office

In early 2003 Andy Hetzel, one of our key associates and a vice president, came to me and suggested that we open a Lansing Michigan office. Lansing is the Michigan state capitol, and Andy felt we could do well there. He had worked in Lansing on the Democratic side for six years and knew a lot of people.

I resisted and told him that other firms based in Detroit had tried in the past—including AMF, Inc.—and they had failed. Andy said, but we will "do things differently." I said fine; prepare a complete business plan along with budget to include staff and office space costs. I suggested he work with our controller.

After about one month, Andy came back with a complete plan including office space, equipment, staff, and how we would be different from past attempts. Andy said we would be staffed by a Democrat *and* a Republican and that we would *not* lobby...which is what the other firms attempted. In this way, we could work with all the lobby firms on public relations projects and not compete with them. He said he also thought he had the Republican, a brilliant young public relations professional who knew Lansing and politics well, who could manage our office.

After much review and conversation, we met Emily Gerkin Palsrok; the Republican that Andy thought could run the office and represent that side of the aisle. Andy would travel to Lansing several times a week—Lansing is ninety miles from our Troy office and represent the Democratic side of the aisle—until we could afford to add a second full-time professional.

We decided to proceed with Emily and opened the JB&A Lansing office in October 2003. Our goal was to lose a minimal amount of money—or invest money—in the first six months of the first year and break even the second six months of the first year. We were wrong. We broke even the first six months, made money the second six months and made money for the first year. We have never looked back and the Lansing office never lost money in any period since its beginning; it continues to do well under the new JB&A owner Lambert Edwards Public Relations – Investor Relations (LEA) ownership. In fact, the office had its best year ever in 2012.

I had an inkling of our potential success when one day early in the operation of the office, I was having coffee with Andy and Emily in Lansing—that is a popular thing for politicians and government employees to do—and there were about thirty people in the coffee shop. Those folks kept nodding or waving or saving hi to either Andy or Emily. I asked them if there was anyone in the room they didn't know. They both looked around the room and pointed out a gentleman sitting alone at a corner table. We walked over and introduced ourselves.

Under the leadership of Emily Gerkin Palsrok, the Lansing office thrived. I was never so proud of them—and JB&A—when we worked with the folks at the Campaign for Smoke-Free Air which was based in Lansing and was designed to eliminate smoking from public places like restaurants and bars throughout the entire state. We worked tirelessly for several years on this effort, and it finally passed, even though only about 19 percent of Michigan's citizens smoked at that time. At the event where Michigan's Governor Jennifer Granholm signed the bill, there was a great "smoke-free" celebration. The Governor asked me if this was the effort of "my" firm. I proudly responded yes. It is the greatest feeling when you can be part of a public relations campaign that helps make society better. And Traffic Safety Now and the Campaign for a Smoke-Free Air are two of the best of my career.

Happy Holidays from the Largest Public Relations Firm in Lansing:

In fall 2005 we took the entire staff to Lansing, Michigan, for a photo on the steps of the State Capitol. Twenty-six people lined up for the photo, which became a JB&A classic. In fact, we used the photo on our Holiday/Christmas card that year and sent it to clients and prospects in the Lansing area marked: *From the Largest Public Relations Firm in Lansing.* We imagined that this infuriated our Lansing competition as we really had about six people in our office there. But the fact remained that if we ever needed all twenty-seven staff members to work on any account or situation, they'd be there, and no one else could say the same. (One person was missing from the photo.)

JB&A Health Care Practice and Technology Practice

We were fortunate to be able to build our practice in these two important categories. They are important and they continue to grow even when the auto industry is down. We worked with the St. John Health System for seven years and helped them through some difficult times. They were a significant client to JB&A.

We also worked with SelectCare for several years and helped them prepare and sell their organization. They called in spring and asked if we could help them prep for the sale by Thanksgiving of that year. I laughed and said you mean next year, which is what happened.

We worked for several years with Sprint PCS and had a fabulous relationship. This client and work got us into the technology category. Sprint PCS worked with several other regional public relations agencies around the country and challenged each firm to "get more positive media coverage" for Sprint PCS than the other firms. JB&A was fortunate to win several of those competitions. Sprint PCS expanded our work responsibilities from Michigan to Northern Ohio and Western Pennsylvania. This work was among our first assignments outside Michigan and paved the way for us to become a national firm based in Michigan. Gayle Joseph headed up our SelectCare and Sprint PCS business.

Foundation Accounts

We had what I called "foundation accounts." These were accounts where our relationship clicked and our professional efforts served the needs of the client if not perfectly, darn close. In all cases we became friends but never took each other for granted and always tried to think outside the box when establishing client/agency goals for the coming year. All of these client/friends were with us for a long time and paid us regularly and had a consistent annual budget. They were the "foundation" of our firm.

Hyundai Motor America

One day in 1998 the phone rang and it was Chris Hosford, director of public relations for Hyundai Motor America with offices in California. They were looking for a public relations agency to provide public relations services for Hyundai in their thirteen-state mid-west region with knowledge of the automotive industry based in Detroit. We had been recommended by Al Vinikour, a friend from the Detroit Press Club. We were no longer working with Buick and expressed our interest. We spent hundreds of hours preparing our presentation, and after a long "pitch" process we were awarded the business.

Everyone who would be part of the Hyundai team took part in the presentation preparation and the presentation meeting, including our youngest team member. This way, Chris Hosford, our potential client, got to meet the entire team he would work with and there would be no surprises later. That win put us on the map...it was the result of building the strongest firm we could and by adding experienced professionals to the account teams to serve our clients. Curt McAllister was the head of our Hyundai business the entire nine years we worked with Hyundai and did a fabulous job. There was no denying the JB&A reputation after that win. We no longer expected to finish second...we were winning business and that would continue.

Blue Cross Blue Shield of Michigan (BCBSM)

Andy Hetzel, the JB&A vice president responsible for present-ing the idea of our Lansing, Michigan, office, was recruited by Blue Cross Blue Shield of Michigan. JB&A had done a significant project for BCBSM headed up by Andy. They were so impressed that they offered Andy a position that was such a great opportunity that even I found it difficult to summon an argument to keep him from leaving our firm. He left JB&A and became vice president for corporate communications at BCBSM, responsible for public relations, adver-tising, and marketing communications. I saw Dan Loepp, the new president at BCBSM at a business conference within that year, and Dan told me how impressed he was with Andy and our firm. He was very positive about the potential for us continuing to work with them although he did not openly commit. I hoped so, and over time, we have continued our relationship with them.

One project all of us at JB&A were all very proud of was the "Blues Cruiser." When Dan took over as president of BCBSM in 2005, he wanted something to show that his company was chang-ing its approach to customer engagement. BCBSM had recently launched new Medicare advantage and Part D coverage plans, and Loepp wanted to signify a "new day" by doing something bold to engage seniors about how Medicare was changing. JB&A presented the idea of the Blues Cruiser—a customized 18-wheel truck painted in BCBSM colors that expanded into a small meeting facility. The Blues Cruiser travelled to state fairs, conferences, and other events to explain Medicare advantage coverage, sign up people to BCBSM plans, and it was designed to be a fun and different happening. BCBSM management approved the idea and the project was chaired at JB&A by Beckie Thompson. From 2006 through 2008, the Blues Cruiser visited 165 cities around Michigan promoting "the new BCBSM." One of my favorite photos was an aerial photo taken of the Blues Cruiser travelling across Michigan's Mackinac Bridge from the

Lower to the Upper Peninsula. In its three years, The Blues Cruiser hosted 58,000 guests and won many awards for BCBSM and JB&A.

R. L. Polk & Co.

Family-owned R. L. Polk & Co. is a foundation account. In the early '90s I had worked for three or four years with R. L. Polk & Co. while at Casey Communications and had gotten to know young Stephen Polk, who was executive vice president then and would eventually take over as CEO of the company. Polk is a great company that provides information to most if not all auto manufacturers, their supporting advertising and public relations agencies, and auto dealers that help them target their consumers.

I had not seen Stephen in a while when I ran into him at an auto industry event. We were both pleased to see each other. He was working with a public relations firm based in New York at the time and asked me when I thought was the last time he had talked with the president of that company. I said I didn't know but guessed six months ago. He said more like two years ago. I said, "That's not good. Can I call you in the morning?" He said yes and we reconnected and began a relationship that has lasts today. I believe the R. L. Polk & Co. is the client we have served the longest at JB&A. They are appreciated by me and everyone at JB&A and now LEA.

One of our first projects after we reconnected with R. L. Polk & Co. was to have the founder, R. L. Polk himself, nominated and eventually elected to the Automotive Hall of Fame. It was a great start to a renewed relationship and friendship.

International Automotive Components Group (IAC)

It is not every day you get to help introduce a new company that has a 160-year legacy in its business. In one case, a new automotive company, after having been divested from another company, contacted us based on our reputation within the auto industry and asked if we could help them communicate their message to their audiences. They gave us the business based on our reputation and presentation to them. We also had no conflicting business.

International Automotive Components Group (IAC) had decades of legacy work in the automotive industry, having been the former interiors division of Lear Corporation, which had acquired numerous interior suppliers over time—one of which even supplied carpet and steering for the Model T, and another that supplied lightweight, durable fabric for President Roosevelt's airplane. IAC was formed in the United States in 2007. Our team helped launch the new organization and position its new executive leadership team, product portfolio, and breadth of services it had established.

Winning and Losing

In the public relations agency business—like in all business—you win some pitches or presentations and you lose some. And it goes in cycles. In good times we felt we could not lose, after winning numerous times in a row. One time we got three new accounts on a Friday...a wonderful way to start the weekend. We would almost always win two out of three times or even three out of four.

Other times winning was tough and our average would be one win out of three or four. It is impossible to know exactly what our winning ratio was over the years, but I estimate it to be around three wins out of five pitches, especially after we got going. Overall, we won more new business than we lost.

It is difficult when you lose a new business opportunity, especially after putting so much into the presentation pitch like we did and feeling so strongly that we could accomplish what the prospect wanted. But it is their decision. I always felt we could have been better at selling...we were great at public relations, but I always felt we could improve our selling. That was my responsibility. I tried to learn more about selling by reading, working with the great professional business coach Barry Demp, and attending sales seminars, etc.

Losing is even more difficult if you lose for the *wrong* reason. But it happens. Know that it will happen and understand that you are not alone. A few of the wrong reasons we heard include:

- We chose the other firm because their CEO or COO went to college with our CEO.
- You had the best presentation and understand our needs, but we chose another firm.
- We chose them because the CEO is my neighbor or relative, etc.
- One time we heard "we chose them because you are too small...another time, because "you are too big."
- We chose them (only) because they are located in New York.
- We chose them because they know more about ___ (add any subject). (This could be true but likely was not.)

I tried to rationalize and say to myself and our team when we lost a pitch that "presenting is like lions, tigers, leopards, and cheetahs on the hunt, in that you are not going to win them all, you just have to win enough." It made us feel better for a minute, but we still hated to lose. Then I would say, "Onward and upward," meaning let's move to the next opportunity.

Finishing Second *Sucks*!

No one wants to finish second. Finishing second sucks. Right? Yes, it absolutely does. But here is a lesson we learned. Finishing second gave us the opportunity to meet new friends. We came close in the bid process and so they liked us. So where we could, we made friends with the people where we finished second. We would seek them and say hello at events, put them on email lists, on Facebook,

LinkedIn and Twitter pages. We did the same with clients that left us as well. We knew that things change. People move from place to place and/or an agency might move on for many reasons. So we kept in touch. We got several new clients from people that had moved on but were impressed with our firm.

Help Eliminate Auto Thefts (H.E.A.T.)

One wonderful example is our friend and long-time very special client Terri Miller. Terri is the executive director of Help Eliminate Auto Thefts, or H.E.A.T. This is a strong organization funded by auto insurance companies and supported by police departments and others to encourage Michigan citizens to report suspicious activities that might be an auto theft.

H.E.A.T. reviews its public relations agency on a regular basis. We bid one year and did a "what we thought anyhow" was a fabulous presentation. We did not get the business but represented ourselves well. It stayed with the incumbent agency. A couple years later we were invited again and bid again…and did *not* get the business again. We decided to never bid on that business again.

One day Terri Miller called me and started out by saying; "John, this is Terri, please don't hang up." She was ready to make an agency change and gave us the business without a new bid (because we had bid twice and she was impressed both times). H.E.A.T. has been a foundation client for years, and Terri has become a good friend. We laugh about her phone call to this day. By the way, auto theft in Michigan has been dramatically reduced in recent years. Way to go, Terri and H.E.A.T.

Moving from Hyundai to VW

Winning the Hyundai business was the foundation upon which we were able to build a strong firm. The experience gained in serving them, the reputation for being a strong automotive public relations firm and the income derived gave us what we needed to move onward and upward. Sort of like in the Stroh days, we had an opportunity to do everything in public relations working with them. They were great, and we became friends with many Hyundai employees, especially Chris Hosford.

In 2007 we became the national agency of record for Volkswagen of America and could no longer work with Hyundai. This was a sad parting because we were very close to the people at Hyundai, knew their products, and really enjoyed working with them for almost nine years. But we had an opportunity to become VW's national agency of record. This meant we'd handle public relations in all of North America and had the potential to have a significantly larger budget. Some might view the decision to leave Hyundai as a mistake, but the move had tremendous potential for our firm and all of us. We all felt it was the right decision for JB&A.

To show how close we were with Hyundai, the first call I made before even considering VW was to Chris Hosford, who was then vice president of Communications at Hyundai. It was gutsy in that just by asking him the question; we would be telling Chris that we were considering not working with him. We stood the chance of him pulling his business from us and we had no assurance that we'd get the VW business. But we were confident he would understand that we'd rather not leave them but had the potential for a larger budget and growth for JB&A. And it was the right thing to do. We talked it over, and even Chris agreed that this was a good move for JB&A. In addition, Chris was not certain how secure our full budget would be in the years ahead. We had helped Hyundai accomplish a lot and were proud of those accomplishments. We made the decision to go after the VW business. It was the toughest decision and gamble I was ever part of, at least at JB&A.

We went through a grueling pitch process and spent a lot of money to distinguish ourselves from the other firms presenting. We hired a professional research firm to research the American public's attitude toward diesel engines. We asked the research firm to give us the research at their cost but guaranteed them that if we were retained by VW, we would work with them on research projects. VW was considering introducing a new generation of diesel engines in North America, and one of our first projects was supposed to be to help introduce that product. The research did separate us from the other firms presenting and we made it to the finals.

Then began a series of meetings and phone conversations over a couple months with the VW purchasing department, all aimed at understanding how we did business and trying to drive the budget down. It was late May and our Hyundai budget would run out at the end of the month, and we had not heard from VW. I was meeting with Beverly Mattinson, our controller, about the very tough decisions we'd have to make if we did not get the business, including cutbacks and layoffs at JB&A. This was a very difficult meeting for Bev and for me.

Curt knocked on my door and said very softly, "We got the VW business." All the negative thoughts were wiped out by those five little words. In an instant the swing of emotion went from crisis to euphoria. I literally cried. We had a meeting with the entire staff and made the announcement by phone conference with the Lansing associates. We were all ecstatic. Our relationship with VW lasted about two years. I wish it could have much more like the Hyundai relationship. Onward and upward.

Shaun Wilson & Associates Public Relations

Shaun Wilson was an associate at JB&A. He was an outstanding practitioner and served clients well. He was and is very strong with media relations, which means working well with the media to place positive stories for his clients. Shaun and I formed Shaun Wilson & Associates Public Relations in 2001. Shaun was the majority owner, and I was the minority owner. We both felt it was the right thing to do. We felt that the timing was good and that we would be successful because of Shaun's many business contacts. I would be senior counsel to any and all of Shaun's clients that needed what I could bring to the table.

Shaun Wilson & Associates Public Relations started well, landing several clients right away. The company had its own office near us in our building at first but eventually moved into downtown Detroit. We had great expectations for the company. Then the economic downturn hit, beginning in late 2007.

Public relations budgets are often reduced during tough economic times. But we learned that minority public relations budgets were not reduced like some were at JB&A—they were eliminated and no new budgets were started. After that stark reality, Shaun Wilson & Associates Public Relations was no more. We both tried hard but the timing was not right. Shaun has a great job with PNC Bank and is doing well to this day.

I will always know that our idea was a good one. It was the right thing to do. I am proud of our effort to start a minority-owned public relations firm.

I have always been a supporter of minorities and their efforts to succeed in business or in anything. From my family history, I did not have any hatred for anyone, and I carry that attitude with me. However, living in northwest Detroit in the 1950's, I had almost no experience with minorities. About the only minorities I saw were bus drivers. I cannot even remember a black person in my high school class, which had over five hundred graduates.

I remember in 1961 when Jake Wood arrived as the first black baseball player for the Detroit Tigers who came up through the Tiger farm system. I was happy because he was a fast runner and a good player. All during the JB&A years, we tried to seek and hire minorities. At one point in 2005, I was very proud that of our staff of twenty-seven, five were minorities and twenty were women.

Takata

Takata did not want to be a major exhibitor at the Society of Automotive Engineers (SAE) show. The SAE show is the largest gathering of automotive engineers in the world; over forty thousand attended this event each year. Curt McAllister, who worked on the Takata business for JB&A, and I devised a plan to get publicity for Takata on the first day of the SAE show. We hosted a Hyge sled test at the Takata facilities in Auburn Hills. A Hyge sled test is conducted to monitor the movement of a weight similar to a vehicle that moves down a track at a high rate of speed and crashes into—in this case—the side of a real car. It is used to test vehicle strength and air bag protection for passengers.

The test was to demonstrate side impact air bags for cars and likely was the first test of its kind to be conducted in front of the automotive press. We packed the Takata test facilities with automotive journalists and conducted the test. The story made the front business page of several Detroit-area daily newspapers and was prominently depicted in several national automotive industry publications. This coverage appeared on the first day of the SAE show and it appeared as if Takata was in the show and that they had the most news on day one. The publicity effort was so successful that the Takata Japanese management was embarrassed even though the plan was approved by the Takata American management in advance. We were told not to be so successful in the future.

The North American International Auto Show

In 2001 we reconnected with Rod Alberts, executive director of the North American International Auto Show (NAIAS) which is the jewel of Detroit and arguably the most significant auto show in North America, if not the world. The NAIAS is sometimes referred to as "The Detroit Auto Show" and is owned by the Detroit Auto Dealers Association (DADA). The DADA is a group of more than two hundred Detroit-area auto dealers. Each January the NAIAS draws more than five thousand automotive media from more than sixty countries and forty states, with over seven hundred thousand visitors to the eleven- or twelve-day gala automotive news event.

I had known Rod since 1989 when two of my clients promoted their products and services at the 1990 NAIAS. These clients were among the first non-automotive companies to participate in the annual major show. Global automotive manufacturers exhibit their new products at the NAIAS in fancy and expensive designer exhibits and seek positive media coverage for their products. The NAIAS is held in Detroit's Cobo Hall and its then over seven hundred thousand square feet. (Cobo Hall is currently expanding and will have more than nine hundred thousand square feet by 2014.) Twenty-five to thirty-five exhibitors position their products in the best light, to gain the best positive media coverage. The NAIAS hosts between thirty-five and forty press conferences each year, introducing as many as sixty new products to the United States and world communities. Thousands of media stories on television and radio, in print, on social media, web sites, etc., feature these products each year.

In addition, the exhibitors entertain media and visitors during the "press days," the first two or three days of the event. The NAIAS annually brings in an estimated $500 million to the Detroit region, so it is huge for the industry and the region. It is among the largest events in any community in the country in sports or entertainment. It is at least comparable to the Super Bowl, World Series, and the Indianapolis 500 race in impact to the local community.

The NAIAS is "Four shows in one:"

1. The Press Days—the first two days—over five thousand automotive journalists attend.

2. Industry Preview Days—the third and fourth days—over thirty thousand automotive engineers attend.
3. Charity Preview Days—the first Friday or fifth day—twelve thousand to fifteen thousand people attend this black-tie children's charity event.
4. General Public Days—the first Saturday through the week from Sunday—as many as 750 thousand members of the general public attend.

During Press Days, the show hosts the thirty to forty press conferences and other important industry events. At the press conferences, auto manufacturers from around the world and the United States introduce their new products and latest technology. There can be from forty to sixty and as many as seventy new car introductions each year.

Industry Preview Days are two days mid-week open to thirty thousand auto industry executives and engineers to attend and "check out" all the new cars in detail.

Charity Preview raises funds through ticket sales for Detroit-area children's charities. Each year, up to 15,000 people attend the "black tie" fund raiser, raising more than $40 million from ticket sales in the last twenty years. It has been called "Detroit's Auto Prom." The 2013 Charity Preview alone raised $3.9 million for the children's charities.

General Public Days are the first Saturday usually through the week from the first Sunday and is open to the general public for a fee.

During our ten years working with the NAIAS, we always enjoyed bringing a national media person from major TV shows like *Good Morning America* or the *Today Show* to the show floor during press days. The media person would reluctantly put on an ID bracelet that allows individuals to move around the show floor and through security. They would think "Why me, this is just Detroit and don't you know who I am? It's just a bunch of cars." When we would take them on the show floor for the first time, they would gasp and exclaim things like, "Holy crap. This is like Hollywood. I had no idea this show was as big and fancy as this." I would smile and say, "Welcome to Detroit, the global center of business news for this week."

Now back to how we got the business. Rod and the executive committee were looking for a partner to help with the local, regional, and national public relations for the NAIAS. We went through the extensive bid process during the spring and summer of 2001 and won the business in October of that year. On November 1, 2001, we began a relationship with the NAIAS—the Detroit Auto Show— that lasted through the 2011 show ending in March of 2011...over ten years and ten shows.

It was a great relationship that positioned us as one of, if not "the" major player in public relations in the region and within the auto industry...just five years after we opened the doors with no clients and no associates. We got to deal with the public relations departments of the entire world's auto companies as well as media from around the world. I always felt this was a very nice plus for the JB&A involvement.

The Top Three Auto Shows in the World Are:

1. Detroit

2. Detroit

3. Detroit

Rod Alberts and the committee do a fabulous job promoting and running the NAIAS. Each year there is a new chairman, and we were fortunate to work with ten chairmen in our years. All members of the committee are Detroit-area auto dealers and take time from their businesses to run the show. They do a fabulous job, with the help of Rod and his staff. Sometimes I think Detroiters take the show for granted. It comes every year just after the holidays. But at least up until now, in my opinion, it is the most significant event in the auto industry in the United States and perhaps even the world. Auto manufacturers make more news in Detroit than anywhere else in the world. I became friends with many of the auto dealers, along with Rod Alberts and his staff.

The NAIAS is so strong that when we researched international and national media one year as to which were the top three auto shows in the world, the NAIAS was number one on just about everyone's list. One journalist said the top three shows in the world are: 1. Detroit. 2. Detroit. 3. Detroit. Many if not all, the manufacturers felt the same way, and the majority said if they could only exhibit at one show, it would be the NAIAS because of the media coverage. ' Each year our JB&A team worked anywhere from two thousand to twenty-five hundred hours on NAIAS public relations activities. Most of these hours would be between December 1 and February 1, but our activities with NAIAS were year-round. All media inquiries from thousands of media came through the NAIAS Public Relations Desk, which was us. It was a tough business challenge to ensure that our pay was enough to allow profitability for JB&A. Our worst year was our first year when we overstaffed the show and invested over four thousand JB&A staff hours serving the NAIAS. But we learned a lot.

The experiences we had working the show were enough to write another book. But mostly our experience working with the global media was of huge benefit to our firm and the individuals working it. But it is tough duty. Many members of our team would spend as many as one hundred hours a week at the show during its run, from December through to the end of January. Imagine walking on cement floors for fifteen hours day for three and four weeks. (It did have carpet over the cement, but you could still feel the cement.)

After the show, our feet always hurt. But the rewards were huge. Not only did we talk with potential new business contacts every day, but we had the opportunity to work with media folks from around the United States and the world and build our reputation with them as well. Nonetheless, working the show for our team would lead to "burn-out" for many of our folks who worked it over the more than ten years we worked with them. And the annual income to JB&A was also nice.

The JB&A NAIAS Team

Our team was headed up by Elizabeth Weigandt for seven shows. Under Elizabeth's direction, we would arrange over four hundred media interviews for the two co-chairs each year, immediately preceding and during the show and thousands of other media stories about the wonderful new products. She said she walked what seemed like hundreds of miles each year meeting camera crews and dashing from exhibit to exhibit, setting up photo ops and interviews and meeting dignitaries. One show year she had a $900 cell phone bill and talked on her phone over ten thousand minutes in one month.

During each show our staff remained in constant contact with the local media to encourage their coverage of the many positive things for the general public to see and do every day at the NAIAS, as this would help drive public attendance. And we had to be ready in case some sort of potential crisis or emergency happened—or someone thought one had happened—so that we could encourage the media to report the facts and not blow it out of proportion. For example, if there was a purse stolen during public days with over seven hundred thousand visitors, or a shoving match, or a smoldering car battery or other kind of battery, or a prank bomb threat, we would contact all news outlets immediately, no matter what time of day or night, with the facts and details and tell them there would be no effect on the remaining days of the show.

If we hadn't done this, their reports could have said there was a "major theft" or "gang fight at Cobo Hall," or "fire at Cobo Hall," or a "bomb threat at Cobo Hall," and such a headline could drive down attendance. This was always an issue to me, especially when our media reported on the weather; after all, it is January in Michigan. The potential of a snowfall coming could impact the next day's attendance, and we all know the chance of getting the snow that is forecast is about 50 percent. So, if there was a slight snowfall forecast, we would get out advisories from the show saying there is no travel problem, come on down, and we would encourage media to report on the roads more often. If there was a major snowfall or other weather condition that would make travel difficult, we got out the alternate show plans to help people plan. Over our years with the show, there were at least eight *"huge"* snowfalls forecast where we got no snow or a dusting.

Working with the Major Automotive Manufacturers:

We also worked with Chrysler, Ford, and General Motors – and all the auto manufacturers' public relations professionals to schedule interviews at their stands at the show for local and national television. We introduced the concept to the committee to measure media coverage of all auto shows in North America. The US manufacturers do this for their products, so we thought it would work for the NAIAS. They measure the amount of positive, neutral, and negative coverage their companies and products receive. The NAIAS media coverage was always more than any other show in the United States. For example, one year we found that the mid-level successful press conference at the NAIAS gained more positive media coverage for the manufacturer than a higher-level news conference at another major show in the United States. Each year these details helped the NAIAS committee show manufacturers that they should make their major intros in Detroit and not somewhere else.

143

Other US shows constantly claimed their media attendance, and therefore coverage, was better than, or as good as, the NAIAS. One show in particular always claimed "huge" media attendance, implying that the media attendance and therefore their potential media coverage was as good as, or greater, than the NAIAS. I checked the media registration for that year and found that the NAIAS had more media from their state alone, than the entire media attending their auto show, based on the estimate of media attending there that we had. The NAIAS welcomes and receives media from over forty states and sixty countries each year.

The Republican Presidential Candidates Tour the NAIAS:

During the 2008 show, the Republican presidential candidates requested entry to the show floor during the press conference schedule. It was my job to work with them to schedule show floor tours where they would be seen by the media *after* the conferences were done at about 5 p.m. If they entered during the conferences, they would disrupt the attention to the products, and the manufacturers would not like this. The NAIAS is for the manufacturers to introduce their products to the world, not to have attending media cover a presidential candidate.

The John McCain campaign team ignored my schedule request and showed up before the press conference schedule concluded. At about 4:15 p.m. or so, I met them in the lobby of Cobo Hall and told them they "only had a short wait before they could enter the show floor at 5 p.m." After some discussion and me politely explaining my position, one McCain official attempted to intimidate me and said in front of me to his committee (McCain was not present, but US Senator Joe Lieberman was), "We will go in anyhow." I said, "No; you need to wait." What he didn't know that I could see was the long line of about twenty NAIAS security guards—many retired Detroit police officers—lined up, blocking the eight doors to the show floor and waiting for direction from me.

I also knew that if I stalled them long enough that the media leaving the show floor or those just arriving would spot Senator Lieberman in the lobby and flock to him for interviews. After several minutes of heated discussion with the McCain group, that is exactly what happened. They held the media briefing outside the show floor. I had won this conflict.

The other candidates and their teams arrived after 5 p.m., and the press conference schedule was completed and was allowed to tour the show floor and get media attention along the way. It was a huge success for the candidates and the car companies.

Another time the CBS show *60 Minutes* came to the NAIAS to do a story on how hard the auto industry was fighting to raise fuel efficiency in all its products. Leslie Stahl, the reporter, balked at getting her "show floor clearance plastic wrist band" but capitulated and entered the show floor. "Oh my, I never expected anything this big," she exclaimed as she looked around the show floor. We took her to the Ford exhibit where two young men were looking at a stylized Ford pickup truck. "Please ask them to leave," she requested. She wanted to film the product and do her story. I think she was implying that those two young men couldn't afford the truck anyhow. I was on duty then and explained that they were both professional National Hockey League players with multimillion dollar contracts, and they most certainly could afford the truck. She waited a few minutes for them to move on and got her story.

During our time working with the NAIAS, I was fortunate enough to travel with several of the auto dealer committee members to the Geneva, Switzerland auto show on four separate occasions. We were to observe how Geneva worked their show to therefore be able to bring what we learned back to the NAIAS. This was truly a great experience. I was also fortunate enough to travel to the Frankfurt, Germany show for another client.

Not in My House, Governor

Another time Michigan's Governor Jennifer Granholm was to tour the show floor one afternoon during the Industry Days, when thousands of engineers are devouring the new competitive products. She would meet individually with top executives of eight manufacturers (OEs) which had a tie to Michigan, pose with that OE's featured new product, and the photos and video would be used for NAIAS publicity and publicity for each of the new vehicles. This program was my assignment for the first several years we worked on the NAIAS. The Governor's Tour got lots of great media coverage each year and helped drive attendance to the public days of the NAIAS.

We had two hours for the governor to spend twelve minutes with each OE, and the additional time was to travel from one exhibit to the next. Each fifteen minutes for the two hours, she was at a different site. It was a tight schedule. We had security and our staff, to ensure movement through the show and its thousands of attendees and workers who all wanted to say hi to the governor. It was no easy task to complete the eight-stop, two hour tour.

After the first stop, the governor's press secretary told me that she and the governor had decided to host a media briefing on the show floor before the second photo session/meeting. The governor would take questions and talk with the media about the news of that day. This could take fifteen to twenty minutes. I informed them that this was not possible, that we had to move or we'd not keep on schedule and might even miss a top executive who had to leave. The press secretary pushed back and said, "We are doing this." I replied, "No you are not, this is my house, and we have a tight schedule and had allotted time at the end of the tour for the media briefing."

We continued on pace and met all of the top execs. The governor met with the media following the tour. She and her team were not happy, but our clients, the automotive manufacturers were—even if they didn't know it.

The more than ten years working with the NAIAS and Rod Alberts is a career highlight for me and JB&A. We made many good friends and good money. However, I am happy that it is over. Rod Alberts is a genius at the way he has grown the show; he and his team have met many, and defeated many, challenges presented by the changing times, down economic conditions, arrival of new media, restricting agreements with the exhibit hall, and so much more. The NAIAS is fortunate to have him. Another aspect of Rod's genius is working with the committee. Each year it changes and sometimes dramatically. The new chairman brings his own brand of management and his own personal style. Some are very easy to work with, some not. But Rod handles it all and does a great job. I always said the NAIAS committee—because of the personalities and audiences—is more political than the political parties.

Rod has numerous audiences he must please. He has a great staff that work extremely hard for the NAIAS. The current committee and especially the current co-chairs are very important. Past committee members can remain active, and Rod needs to respect and listen to them all. Then he has the unions and management at the Cobo Hall facility, where the NAIAS is held, that he has to respect and serve. He has the governor's office and the mayor's office to respect and serve. Then there are the four to six thousand media that cover the show, some year round and, others just during the January event. Then there are the exhibitors and sponsors, many of which are not auto companies. But the most important audience is the automotive manufacturers who exhibit each year. The show is for them to show off their products first to the media, then the industry engineers, and then the general public. And each of these entities believes they are the most important audience. Rod has a tough assignment, but he does it well.

My personal goal was for JB&A to work with the NAIAS for ten shows, which we did. We began work with the NAIAS November of 2001 and concluded in March of 2011. We wish Rod, the committee, and the NAIAS the very best. It is a Detroit and auto industry institution.

Rod sent me the following email just preceding the first NAIAS we were not part of:

John:

I hope to see you down here (at the show). You have had everything to do with the success we have had and are having today. Great years together!

Thanks my friend,
Rod

Up until 2006 our auto industry business was 55 percent of our total business at JB&A. I learned from many professionals and PRSA industry examples to try not to let any one client or industry dominate your client roster or you will be in trouble if anything should happen to that client or industry.

But we were doing so well in the auto industry that this segment grew to about 70 percent of our business at JB&A. Even though there is a danger in doing so, you just can't turn down new business no matter what industry it comes from, and we were not going to turn down auto business, so that category grew as did our health care business.

Many of the JB&A Clients

We worked with what we called the bluest of the blue chip companies based in the region, often serving them nationally. Some of our ongoing clients included:

- ACCESS (Arab Community Center for Economic and Social Services)
- Accident Fund
- America's Thanksgiving Day Parade (Detroit)
- American House
- American Plastics Council
- Ameritech Cellular
- Area Agency on Aging 1-B
- ASC (formerly American Sun Roof)
- Automation Alley
- Automotive Bright Products Association
- Automotive Hall of Fame
- Automotive Interiors Show
- Automotive Multimedia Interface Collaboration (AMIC)
- Automotive Youth Educational Systems (AYES)
- Bartech
- Black Book
- Blue Cross Blue Shield of Michigan
- Borgess and Foote Hospitals
- Buick Motor
- Campaign for Smoke Free Air
- Chartered Financial Analysts Society of Detroit
- Continental Automotive
- Dealer Concepts
- Delphi Automotive
- DuPont Automotive
- DuPont Performance Elastomers
- DTE
- Eagle Ottawa Leather
- Federal Mogul
- Food Bank Council of Michigan
- Ford Motor Credit

- Great Lakes Crossing
- Harbour Consulting (now Oliver Wyman)
- HB Stubbs
- Harley Ellis Devereaux
- Harris Interactive
- Health Care Association of Michigan
- Healthy Kids Healthy Michigan
- Henkel Automotive
- Help Eliminate Auto Thefts (H.E.A.T.)
- Hike It for Health (tobacco tax campaign)
- Hyundai Motor America
- Honigman Miller
- Infomedia
- International Automotive Components Group (IAC)
- Kelly Services
- Kmart Corporation
- KPMG
- Life Secure
- Marshall Fields/Macy's
- McCann Erickson Advertising
- McCarty Cancer Foundation
- McCormick and Schmick's Restaurant, Troy
- MEDC
- Michigan Association of Area Agencies on Aging
- Michigan Association of Community Mental Health Boards
- Michigan Association of Public School Academies (MAPSA)
- Michigan Association of United Ways
- Michigan Flocking Association
- MSXI
- Oakland University
- Osram Automotive Lighting
- Osram Opto Semiconductors
- Port Huron Hospital

- Pricewaterhouse (before Coopers)
- Re/Max
- Reynolds and Reynolds
- Right Management Consultants
- R. L. Polk & Co.
- SAE Detroit
- SAE World Congress Expo
- Saleen Automotive
- Salvation Army of Detroit
- Scenic Michigan
- SelectCare
- Siemens
- Special Olympics of Michigan
- St. John Health System
- Spaulding DeDecker Associates
- Sprint PCS
- Subaru
- Sverdrup
- T-Systems
- Tenneco Grand Prix of Detroit
- Trinity Health System
- The North American International Auto Show (NAIAS)
- Visteon
- Volkswagen of America
- Walbro Automotive

2007 Results

Back at JB&A, we had our eleventh consecutive year over year record in 2007 and were poised for a fabulous year in 2008. Our net income was $3.3 million and gross sales had gone well over $4 million for the first time. Since our first year of 1996, we had increased our business each year over the last. We were now a $4 million firm, accomplished in under ten years.

In 2005 we had our office redone with new carpeting in all hallways, new ceiling throughout, new lighting, new paint throughout, a new lobby area and furniture, and new artwork, and we had added another 1,700 square feet and a new conference room and table and chairs. Most of the work was done at no cost to us by the building management company in an effort to have us sign a new seven-year lease. We all originally wanted to leave the Top of Troy, now PNC building, but with what we were offered, and ten months' free rent, even those most determined to move decided that we should stay. Our lease rate of the length of the seven year lease would be lower than the rate we had been paying in the previous lease. And we were doing so well that the management company gave us right of first refusal for any additional space on floor. The colors in our office were eye-catching, and we received numerous complements from clients and visitors. We called it "Bailey blue."

I had been recognized by George W. Bush which gave me—and therefore the firm—outstanding community exposure. More on "W" later.

But here's the lesson for everyone. Even though our lease rate was in the $19 to $21 per square foot range, it could have been lower at another lesser building in not quite as prime a location. Also, just about everyone at JB&A had a private office which drove up square footage and many had windows. At the time it *was* the correct thing to do, but a business leader must keep costs down. Could we have had more open spaces and therefore less square footage? Yes. Could we have been in another less expensive yet very professional building? Yes. I knew of other public relations firms in the region that were paying in the $11 to $14 range per square foot. That folks would equal—with less overall square footage—a 50 percent savings on space in the last seven years of the lease. Roughly speaking, that would mean an expenditure of about $900,000 versus $1,800,000. Hindsight is perfect vision. I use these figures to help you make these decisions as you grow your business.

Lessons Learned: *Try not to under - or overestimate yourself. That is going to be hard to do, but you must constantly evaluate where you are and where you are going. Ask and listen to your advisors.*

CHAPTER 15

THE 2008 RECESSION

During our annual two-day off-site management planning meetings with our management team, we projected continued growth and set our numbers very conservatively. We expected conservatively $3.6 million net sales in 2008 and $5 million gross again and were considering expansion to other cities, specifically Grand Rapids and Chicago. Our controller and I thought we really had a chance to hit $4 million in net sales in 2008. Our Lansing office expansion was a huge success and we expected that to continue into other cities, but we knew we'd have to go slow so as not to over-commit.

Then the national news warned of very rough times ahead. US auto sales, which had been at around 16 million units in 2007, were now projecting downward and no one knew how low. It turns out that auto sales went below 9 million units in 2008 and stayed there for 2009—about a 50 percent decline. Our auto supplier clients were hit particularly hard as they were producing parts for the 16 or 17 million units and had built up huge inventories. Simply stated, they stopped production and laid off thousands. The entire community and country was in panic, banks were in trouble due to a loan crisis, and there was a national mortgage crisis; things were not looking too good for anyone. The recession had hit us all.

JB&A did not lose any clients due to the recession, but most of our auto clients cut their budgets dramatically. One auto client, for example, went from a budget of more than $200,000 annually to $8,000 in 2008. We lost about half our auto budget in 2008, and at that time, auto was about 70 percent of our business. This meant more than $1.2 million in lost net revenue for JB&A. Instead of hitting the very realistic $3.6 million net sales, it would be more like $2.4 million net sales, or less. We were still a strong company and did not lose any business or budget from our non-automotive clients, but we had to make some tough decisions.

I have stated that we were also very strong in the other categories of health care, public affairs, and technology. These categories continued to provide growth for our firm and helped us survive the economic downturn.

By May 2008, 70 percent of our business was reduced by half, and we needed to adjust. Suddenly, we had too many people and too much space. We reduced staff by two public relations professionals and one administrative person. We cut budgets anywhere we could and froze salaries and hiring for what ended up to be one year. Natural attrition took a couple more public relations professionals. I took a 40 percent pay cut that lasted through the entire recession. I was not happy with my pay cut but knew that it was important to maintain a strong staff and would last at least until we could regain our growth mode.

We asked the building management if we could give back the 1,700 square feet of space we had added two years before—which we no longer needed. They were not interested. We asked for a break in our monthly rent, which was then about $21,000 per month… they said no but did offer to let us miss a few months' rent with those amounts becoming loans to JB&A…which we declined. We tried to play tough with them by saying that if they did not reduce our rent to $12,000 monthly that we could go out of business. (I set the $12,000, thinking they might counter at $15,000.) They did not budge. The building management executive we reported to said to us, "JB&A has been so well run and has such a strong reputation, that we know you will work out of this tough spot." They also said they could not set a precedent by doing this, as other tenants would want the same and they could not afford it. They were smart.

What I did accomplish which saved us $126,000 over the remaining life of the lease was to find a sub-tenant for space we were no longer using. We had hired a real estate broker to help us find a potential tenant, but our sub-tenant came from, once again, my contacts and this time through the Troy Chamber of Commerce. That tenant stayed with us for the rest of our lease at the PNC Building.

Our non-automotive clients were strong and continued to grow. We did survive the recession.

Comerica Bank

Mark Twain is attributed as saying:

"Banks are fair weather friends. A banker gives you an umbrella when the sun is shining and wants it back when it is raining."

I always laughed at this quote until the day in October 2008 when our Comerica bank representative called and said, "We can no longer work with you. By the end of next month, you will need to find a new bank." Twain's quote was not funny anymore. At first I thought the guy was kidding. I laughed at what he said. We had had a line of credit, which most companies do, which helps maintain a smooth cash flow, since our first years in business. In addition, Comerica had been my personal bank since my teenage years, which was like forty years by then. We never had a problem with the bank, always paid on time, and we were often far below the ratio of loan to accounts receivables they require and sometimes we owed nothing and never wrote a bad check, nothing.

I understand their position. We are a service company. Our assets are our people, ideas, goodwill, and reputation. You can't put a lien against those things. We had no hard assets like a building or equipment and much of our business was in the hard-hit automotive category. Any electronics we had were—as you know—out of date the day we received them. And during the economic crunch, "unsupported loans" were the cause of many banks getting themselves in trouble. But I still kept hearing radio commercials saying that Comerica was "the bank for small business." Yeah, right, but not *our* small business.

So we began the search for a new bank. This is not an easy task. Bev Mattinson worked many hours on this effort. We located Mercantile Bank out of Grand Rapids, who agreed to work with us. But now I had to personally guarantee the loans and maintain a balance of $50,000 in savings with them. Again Janet and I talked. The bank wanted a $120,000 lien against our Rochester Hills, Michigan home but we offered our northern Michigan home as collateral. After a valuation review of our northern home, they agreed, and we proceeded. Thank goodness we had a new bank, but now I had the added pressure of knowing that our vacation dream home had a lien against it. That sucked and led to a new level of worrying on my part and loss of sleep. But JB&A move onward and upward.

Ethics: Honesty is the Only Policy

I have always been a supporter of ethics in business and personal life. Maybe it was my mom and dad, in addition to all the problems I saw clients get into throughout my career, or my habit of following the news every day to see which prominent person or company was in trouble or—maybe it was just me. It seems like I am going against the American way by saying all this because politicians will all tell you they like blue, for example if you like blue, and they will tell someone else they like red or green, etc., etc. But I had seen too many men, women, and companies, etc. get into a big mess by not being truthful and ethical.

My own personal code of ethics is simple: *honesty is the only policy*. When in doubt, use this gut check test and ask yourself:

- If what I just did (or neglected to do) was immediately reported on Twitter and in the world's media would it embarrass my organization, my family or me?
- Would I tell my children to do the same thing?
- Would I share my decision with my mother?

In later years I would write and speak on the subject to general audiences and audiences of public relations professionals. I wrote blogs and wrote for newspapers, both general and professional, on the subject. I registered MisterEthics so I could use that name. Quoting Mark Twain, my favorite author again,

"Always tell the truth, you'll never have to remember what you said."

Jeff Lambert

In late 2008 one such speaking opportunity came my way when the Grand Rapids, Michigan Chapter of PRSA invited me to speak to their chapter on the subject of ethics. Off I went to Grand Rapids to speak to about eighty to one hundred public relations profession- als. Jeff Lambert was in the audience. He was and is the CEO and owner of Lambert, Edwards & Associates Public Relations · Investor Relations (LEA), based in Grand Rapids. I had met Jeff before and we chatted after the lunch presentation and he invited me to visit

159

their offices in Grand Rapids. LEA was smaller than JB&A in 2007 by a couple hundred thousand dollars but was more profitable, was growing nicely, and was not impacted much—at least not like we were—by the recession.

Jeff and I recognized that we were very similar firms in most aspects. Our firms had very little, if any, competing businesses, we always wanted to expand to Grand Rapids, and they always wanted to expand to Detroit. They always wanted to be in the automotive space, where we were strong, and we always wanted to be in the investor relations side of the business, where they were strong. They had some business in Lansing but no office, and of course, we had a thriving office there. They even banked with Mercantile Bank, our new bank. At the very least, we might be able to provide office space to LEA in Lansing. Both firms were located in Michigan but served many clients nationally. The only major difference was in the ages of the CEO/owners of our companies. Jeff was thirty-seven; I was seventy. Humm, we both thought to ourselves. We agreed to keep in touch.

CHAPTER 16

WHO WILL SUCCEED JOHN BAILEY AT JB&A?

Since I founded JB&A in 1996, I knew the day would come when I would need to begin to step aside. Heck, I might even want to step aside. I have always had lots of energy and knew I could remain active in the business community well past sixty-five years old, the "sort of" retirement age for Americans. My goal was to develop my replacement, a woman or man who could take over JB&A. My kids were not in the public relations field so that was not an option.

At different times over the years, I had three people in mind as that person. There was and is no question in my mind that any of those three could have done a fabulous job as CEO of JB&A. Even after I sold the firm, I know any of them could have done the job. If this worked, I would begin to back away, taking less salary and giving up ownership for ten years until I was gone and JB&A had a new owner.

But life happens, and none of them for their reasons wanted the job when I was ready to begin the process. All three were and are great public relations professionals and would have done well, and I would have enjoyed working with any of them well into the future. So I began looking at other options for the future of JB&A. There were three, as I discussed with my CPA/accountant, Rob Dutkiewicz, and my attorney, Jeff Levine. Both these professionals have been with me since day one of JB&A and knew me and the company well. The options were:

1. Go out of business

2. Continue to seek a replacement from within

3. Seek a buyer for JB&A

Option one was never considered. I had tried number two since the beginning and this had not worked. That left the third option: seek a buyer for JB&A.

In 2006 I hired a national public relations merger and acquisition consulting business (M&A) to help me find a buyer for JB&A. I paid a significant amount up front and the M&A company would get a significant percentage from a sale. They did a complete review of all our activities and ranked them, comparing us to small, medium, and large public relations firms around the United States. They ranked things such as profitability, operations, sales, client base, percent of client business in any category, percentage of billability of each associate, percentage of billability by the company overall, and more.

All in all, they ranked us in twenty-six business categories. We did well in most operations categories, but were not as billable as other firms and therefore were not as profitable as other firms…yet we were profitable. This goes back to what I said earlier, what do you want in the area of profits? My decision was less profit but more associate buy-in and appreciation of what we were doing and what their role was in the company. But now as I looked for a buyer, this lower-profit decision had become an issue with a potential new buyer.

My consultant and I narrowed the search down to four firms, all of them based outside Michigan. We had talked to six, but most firms did not want to be in Detroit, wanted more profits, and/or were afraid of the auto industry and our role in it. So that did not work.

I also met with owners of two other Michigan-based firms to discuss a merger or acquisition but neither worked. Here I caution you in any merger to be sure of chemistry between firms and be sure the other firm is as financially strong as you are...stronger if possible. One of the potential merger candidates would not have been a good fit, and the other was seeking to take unfair advantage of our client base, and accounts receivables and would likely have driven us out of business immediately after the closing. You could say I almost made the same mistake two different times. The key word here is "almost."

Lambert, Edwards & Associates Public Relations · Investor Relations

In January of 2009, there was a press release issued by Jeff Lambert at Lambert, Edwards & Associates Public Relations · Investor Relations, stating they had had another very successful year over the previous year and were looking to expand into the Detroit market and would consider an acquisition of a public relations firm in the Detroit market. I don't know if Jeff was targeting me with that announcement, but he might as well have. I called Jeff immediately and expressed interest, and this began a series of meetings that led to the eventual sale of JB&A to a financially strong public relations-investor relations firm that *wanted* to be in Detroit, *wanted* to be serving the automotive industry, had similar corporate culture and little if any conflicting client business, and had grown in 2008 and were now larger than JB&A.

Jeff and I knew our firms were compatible. And I was looking to get out from under the financial burden the bank had placed on us. We still had little or no competing business as clients. We met several times and then Jeff did something very much like what I would have done if the situation were reversed. He asked me exactly what I wanted from the sale. Then he asked me to write everything down. How much money you would like from the sale, what timing do you want, everything that is in your mind, and be open and honest...which was easy for me to do.

I worked hard on the document for several days. Of course, I already had been thinking of what I wanted and needed. I presented the document to Jeff, and after a day of reviewing it, he said, let's proceed. And that document became our letter of agreement. This is a lesson to you all too. I was reasonable. Not only did I list what I wanted, but I tried to put myself in Jeff's position, that is, what is fair—what is best not only for John and JB&A, but what is fair for Jeff and LEA. By honoring my desires from the sale of JB&A, Jeff showed me what kind of honorable professional and businessman he is, and I hope he felt the same about me. He must have, as he used the document to create our final letter of agreement. In July we signed an agreement to close the sale on September 30, 2009.

I was pleased because I could save the jobs of many JB&A staffers and could therefore continue the relationship with so many excellent clients. And I was also pleased because of our financial agreement; I could pay off the lien and be free and clear with the bank. And at seventy years of age, to me, that was important. If I had been Jeff's age, I might have requested that we merge and keep both names in some way because I would have many years to pay off the lien myself. We also agreed to keep the JB&A name for at least one year. We did, and one year after we signed the deal, we changed the name to Lambert-Edwards Public Relations - Investor Relations and I was still with the company.

People ask me if I am sorry to see the name JB&A go away. After all, it was my baby, so to speak. In a way it is hard, but it was the best option for me and the firm and my family. The JB&A name will live on in the hearts and minds of everyone who worked for and/or with us in those years. I know it will with me.

President George W. Bush, Forty-Third President of the United States of America

I always loved working with the news media, and I think they enjoyed their relationship with me as well. Whether in media training, crisis communication, selling a story, or developing media strategy, I was and still am very good. I always tried to help them do their job and get a good story while keeping my clients in positive focus in their minds. I made lots of good friends in the media too, most especially Tom Walsh, business editor then business columnist of the *Detroit Free Press*. Carol Cain, also of the *Free Press* and CBS and WWJ TV is also a friend of mine.

One day Carol called to ask about my company, which was celebrating its ninth anniversary. She asked me what I owed my/our success to, and I said hard work, an unrelenting quest for more— service to clients and income from them. I told her one of the reasons I left my previous job was because the new owners were not impressed with me and thought I was too old as they were promoting people who were in their thirties for the most part. This company was headquartered in London with its US base in New York City. Janet had told me she thought they were ignoring me and my potential, and at age fifty-seven, I knew I did not fit their mold. I told this all to Carol and she wrote a very nice story about me and our firm, which appeared in the Sunday *Detroit Free Press*.

A week later on February 7, 2005, in the morning, my assistant came to me and said, "The White House in on the phone." I laughed and joked, "How can the White House be on the phone?" I thought it was one of my golf buddies playing a joke. I thought about Rob Falls, out of Cleveland, who would do something like this. I almost answered the phone, "Hi Rob."

I took the call and the voice said, "I am a speech writer for President George W. Bush, and we'd like to know if you would let us use your story when the president comes to Detroit next week to talk to the Detroit Economic Club." He said if used, my story would be an example of the spirit of entrepreneurship. "Of course," I said, and he replied that there was no guarantee and he'd be back in touch. Later that morning, someone else called and asked for personal information (to do a background check), but that person still did not know if it would be used. They asked if I was planning on being at the luncheon in two days. I said, "I am now."

I called Beth Chappell, President and CEO of the Detroit Economic Club (DEC) and asked if she could get me in. I was a member of that organization and often sat on the dais. She said they were sold out with more than 1,500 business women and men expected to attend. I explained the situation and she said, "You'll be at the head table." It showed me again how important knowing someone and being involved is.

The Detroit Economic Club is recognized as one of the top three speaking venues in the United States. Many presidents and major CEOs have spoken there before and will again.

I still did not know if my info would be used. I decided not to tell anyone—except Janet of course—because I would have been embarrassed if it were not used.

So, I went to the DEC lunch. The attendees were to eat first and then the president would arrive and deliver his speech at noon. Because it was so special, the speech was televised. It took an extra two hours to get in to the lunch because of security checks. I saw people throwing away good writing pens because they were not allowed. Beth escorted me to my seat on the dais and asked if I knew anything. I said no, and that I hoped she might. She knew nothing.

I finished my lunch, and there was about twenty-five minutes until the president was expected to arrive. Then Beth came up to me and said, "Come with me." She escorted me to a reception room, and there were five men there: Rick Wagoner, then Chairman of General Motors; William Ford, Jr., Chairman of the Ford Motor Company; Dieter Zetsche, then Chairman of then DaimlerChrysler Corp.; James Nicholson, CEO of PVS Chemicals, Inc., and Saul

Anunzis, then Chairman of the Republican Club of Michigan... and *me*. I figured something might be up. We all stood around for ten minutes or so, when an athletic-looking guy about 5 11 came bouncing around the corner and said, "Hi, I'm George Bush." I was the first one he met. We shook hands and had our picture taken. This lasted about one minute for each of us.

We returned to our seats, and President Bush was introduced. He began his talk and went on and on about the American Spirit and working hard and not giving up. Thirty-five or forty minutes later, nothing had been mentioned, and I was thinking at least I got to meet him, when he said, "John Bailey is with us." I couldn't believe it. He then talked about me and my business, my wife, my goals, and how from nothing, we were one of the largest public relations firms in Michigan. He mentioned—I have always liked to say—all my key messages about life, my business, and he complimented my wife. It was awesome. Here is what the president said:

No one knows the power of ownership better than American entrepreneurs. John Bailey is with us. It's an interesting story about entrepreneurship and optimism.

Nine years ago, after a life in public relations, he found himself trapped in a company that offered no hope for advancement. His wife—sounds like a pretty straight-forward woman, I'm about to quote her—kind of reminds me of Laura.

She said, "What part of the writing on the wall can't you understand? They don't want people over fifty." This is what the wife was telling John.

He didn't get discouraged. He responded in true American fashion. He went out and founded his own firm. And today, John's business is one of the largest public relations firms in Michigan.

And here's what he had to say, "It's very daunting to go out there. But I learned it can be done, that hard work and strong ethic pays." He went on to say, "It sounds corny, but good guys can finish on top."

The dream of a hopeful America is to say that if you work hard and dream big no matter who you are, you can finish on top. Thanks for letting me come. God bless.

My mobile phone began to buzz even before I left the dais. Friends and family began calling and wishing me well and wanting to know how it all happened. I was interviewed by the media numerous times about the speech and how this all happened in the days that immediately followed President Bush's speech. Even years later people mention it as if it were yesterday. It was certainly a career highlight—maybe "the" career highlight.

As you can imagine, I received many notes, emails, and calls of congratulations. It was a wonderful experience. But one call I received stood out. If was from a nurse just over fifty years old who had been terminated that day after twenty-six years with the same hospital system. She was crying and saying "I love this place; how could they do this?" I asked her if she had a college degree. "Oh, yes, I am an RN and have a master's degree." I told her that the health care field is growing rapidly, and that she would be able to start her own company, or find a job and likely a better one where she might even make more money. And that people like her were—and are—in great demand. She was very thankful and felt much better. I never heard from her again, but I am positive she is doing well.

Lessons Learned: *Always treat the media professionally and honestly. They will take care of you. Believe it when someone tells you, "The White House is calling."*

Michigan Governor Jennifer Granholm (L), Janet Bailey, and John at the 2006 North American International Auto Show. The event is called Detroit's prom.

The JB&A team on the steps of the Michigan State Capitol; only one person was missing that day. The photo was used for the 2005 holiday card from The Largest Public Relations firm in Lansing to our Lansing clients and prospects. Photo courtesy Dave Trumpie Photography.

John (R) and Mike Devilling, JB&A Executive Vice President

The great Blues Cruiser sponsored by Blue Cross Blue Shield of Michigan. The Blues Cruiser travelled all across Michigan visiting 165 cities along the way. BCBSM wanted to show it was changing its approach to customer engagement under its new president. The Blues Cruiser did that. Here it is shown crossing Michigan's Mackinac Bridge between Michigan's Upper and Lower Peninsulas. Dale Fisher photo ©.

Family and friends helped me celebrate the Wayne State University Career Award presented by the Communications department. Here are four former JB&A associates: L to R, Andy Hetzel, Hope Brown, Beckie Thompson, me, and Emily Gerkin Palsrok.

Likely the pinnacle of John's career came in February 2005, when he was highlighted in a speech by President George W. Bush. President Bush was in Detroit to talk to over one thousand members of the Detroit Economic Club about the "spirit of American entrepreneurship" and used John starting JB&A as an example.

John J. Bailey at the time of rapid growth at JB&A.

CHAPTER 17

MY THREE-YEAR PHASE-OUT AT JB&A

My deal with Jeff Lambert called for me to work full time but with annually tapering weekly hours for three years after we signed the agreement in 2009. After the first six months or so, I called Jeff and requested that I work fewer hours, more like twenty per week, and that my salary be reduced accordingly. He laughed—I don't know if he ever had someone ask for a salary reduction—and he agreed. Then in March of 2011, Janet and I were in Arizona with friends when we met a retired couple who asked us why we were still working. I could not sleep that night and called Jeff when I returned with another salary reduction request. I told Jeff I did not want office hours and would keep up with company activities through email and did not want any salary. He laughed again and agreed.

I did some good things during those three years. I introduced Jeff to Josh Linkner who is part of Dan Gilbert's team rebuilding downtown Detroit. I don't know if meeting Josh helped Jeff get the space LEA eventually moved into in downtown Detroit, but it didn't hurt. I also helped win the business of a major Detroit organization that in my opinion has the potential to become one of the largest clients on the LEA Detroit roster. That's up to LEA now. I also introduced LEA to the management at a major health system, and we did presentation training with them, and this organization could also become a major client on the roster.

I remained active on three boards including the Detroit Regional Chamber, the Automotive Hall of Fame, and the Woodward Avenue Action Association and continued to introduce LEA to my contacts. I resigned those boards in fall of 2012. But I tried to introduce LEA people to key leaders in the hopes that one of them could replace me on these boards. Gayle Joseph has been invited on the Automotive Hall of Fame Board which should show the world that she is a player in the automotive space.

LEA hosted a retirement party for me at Hockey Town Café in downtown Detroit on October 17, 2011. We invited about 120 people from my family and my past at Stroh, Casey, Franco, and of course, JB&A. More than one hundred attended. It was a great evening and I thanked everyone.

My last day in the office was Thursday of that week after my final Detroit Regional Chamber board meeting. I came to the office for a couple hours. After lunch I walked around the office again and listened to pieces of conversations. They were great and once again, they did not need me. I felt like I had done my job, and I left the office for the last time. It was really strange. I couldn't look back, only forward. I was walking out of the company I started and built with so many others…never to return as an associate. I felt like I was walking on a cloud. The JB&A chapter was over for me. But it was time and I was seventy-three years old.

I am proud of Jeff and current staffers who have moved our office from Troy to downtown Detroit. It was something I always wanted to do. They've done it. I expect great things for Detroit and LEA, especially if they remember to serve those clients well.

CHAPTER 18

MY HOME TOWN

Detroit, Michigan, and People

If you couldn't tell already, I love Detroit and Michigan. It hurts me when I hear negative talk about my town and my state. We do have our problems and are working to solve them, but following is a list of communities and states that do not have problems:

I am so grateful for those people who are making a difference in our town. Thank you to Mike Ilitch, Dan Gilbert, Roger Penske and the companies that have returned downtown, including Blue Cross Blue Shield of Michigan. And thank you to those who have remained downtown, like DTE, and so many others. It is now time for the rest of us to join them and go downtown and spend time and money. I am proud of Jeff Lambert for moving his (our) company downtown. It is happening, folks.

But I can't forget those people and companies that went before us, like The Stroh Brewery Company and Peter W. Stroh and the Stroh family. And the Kresge Foundation and the Manoogian family. Thank you all.

The Detroit Regional Chamber

The Detroit Regional Chamber (DRC) was the one organization that offered me a lot. I joined to meet people and help my community...Detroit.

I joined in the mid-1970s while at AMF, Inc. Tony would often ask me to represent him and the company at events, including its Mackinac Policy Conference. My association with The Stroh Brewery Company was an added benefit. I should point out that my first two "Mackinac Policy Conferences" were on cruises, one down the Mississippi River and one from Miami to Newfoundland, Canada. After those, the DRC moved the conferences to wonderful Mackinac Island and held meetings at the historic Grand Hotel. My goal when I joined the DRC was to be an insider and member of its board of directors. It took me thirty-four years, but I never gave up and made it when I was appointed to the 2009 board.

In the meantime, I was very active in the DRC and served on numerous committees, including the Committee for a Safer Greater Detroit and as a member of the board of trustees of Leadership Detroit. I met lots of people in those years which helped me build my network and my reputation and I became friends with three DRC presidents: Frank Smith, Richard Blouse, and Sandy Baruah.

The DRC's Leadership Detroit (LD)

I was a member of LD XIII that graduated in 1992. Leadership Detroit is a ten-month program, one or two days a month, where sixty-five people go through a course to understand the community, its problems, its strengths, and its weaknesses. The purpose is to develop people who understand the issues and therefore can help make a difference. I can't say enough positive things about this program. Once again, the DRC was offering me the chance to meet important community leaders while learning more about my community and how I might be able to help.

One special committee I served on was part of a committee on diversity. We laughingly called ourselves a mini "Noah's Ark" as we "had one of everything" on our nine-person committee. (We didn't really, but it felt like it.) We had at least one: Asian, Hispanic, African American man and woman, gay, lesbian, white female, and me representing white males. We met periodically and each shared life experiences. Our talks were very open and frank.

This was one of the most moving and rewarding experiences of my life. And it worked; we all learned a better appreciation of each other. Those people became very special to me, and to this day, they are my brothers and sisters.

Everyone should have the opportunity to share such a wonderful experience.

The DRC's Mackinac Policy Conference

This annual three-day event held on Mackinac Island in late May is one of the highlight business events of the year. Business women and men and their spouses and/or significant others, along with Michigan elected officials, attend the conference. Most of the time, the event sells out, and between 1,800 and 2,000 people pack the Grand Hotel and the island for the sessions that discuss the important issues of the time, which are supposed to lead to solutions in Detroit and Michigan.

The DRC brings in many fine speakers with national and international reputations who address the issues from their perspective. There are numerous discussion sessions each of the three days and often lunch and dinner speakers of national repute.

But to me, and research of attendees agrees, the number one thing to do on the island is to network. I would attend with an agenda to meet so many people and to see if I could set a meeting for the following weeks to discuss public relations.

At JB&A we were part of the initial move toward business research leading up to the conference that gained media coverage and promoted the conference itself. In the beginning a few media people attended, but now the conference is attended by many media outlets and is a major source of news during the time leading up to the conference as well as during the conference.

It is difficult for someone going to the conference for the first time; you won't know many people and don't know how to maximize your opportunity, but you learn. After I attended numerous conferences—I've attended about thirty—I knew the ropes and would often only attend the sessions I was most interested in or the speakers I really wanted to hear.

If I missed a session or two, people would kiddingly tell me I should go to the sessions. One time a friend of mine and I decided to miss several hours and go golfing. Everyone was on us, saying you're going to miss this and that, but we went anyhow. Guess who did the same and took the same carriage with us to the golf course? Detroit Mayor Dennis Archer and Wayne County Executive Ed McNamara. We chatted for forty-five minutes and got to know those two important leaders even better and they us.

In 2009, the second to last conference I attended, with sponsorships, networking, client, and prospect meetings, my staff and I had me booked for nineteen meetings during one day, and I made them all. Someone asked me if I had a drink at each one…I'd have no chance of survival if I had.

I attended my last conference in 2010, and my name tag included ribbons signifying that I was a: Board Member, LD Graduate, Sponsor, Speaker, and Political Action Committee supporter. Paul W. Smith made fun of my name tag with so many ribbons on his morning show on the WJR-AM air—which was good exposure for me and my firm. I was finally an insider.

Overall, attending the Mackinac Conference gave me another opportunity to build my network and reputation and to stay connected with those I had already met.

The Troy Chamber of Commerce

Most companies and individuals will benefit from joining a local chamber of commerce. I know I did. Again, I met lots of wonderful people and continued to build my network. But you have to work at it. Just joining is not enough. The more effort you put into any membership, the more you will receive from it.

After a couple years, I was fortunate to be appointed to the board of directors at this chamber. Troy, Michigan is a northern suburban community of Detroit with 85,000 residents and many major businesses. The Troy Chamber of Commerce represents about eight hundred local businesses and is very active in the community and never backs away from an issue and always stands for what was right in that community. After serving in the various chairs, including treasurer and vice chairman, I was honored to serve the Troy Chamber as Chairman of the Board for the last half of 2007 and all of 2008 and to work with its dynamic president at that time, Michelle Hodges. In this organization, as with the Detroit Regional Chamber, I would speak on panels on public relations and entrepreneurship which linked me to even more businesses.

In all business or professional organizations that I served, my goal was to provide strong leadership to that organization and to make a difference to them. I also wanted people to know that I was a public relations professional and that if ever they, or anyone they knew, wanted public relations services, that I would be honored to be included on the list of firms they might consider. Or, they could hire us directly.

I wasn't as good a salesman as Tony Franco, but my network was broader and stronger. It did lead us to numerous business opportunities over the years.

The Public Relations Society of America – Detroit Chapter

I joined the PRSA-Detroit in the late 1960s. I was always told that it is important to give back to your profession. So I became active and eventually was asked by Robert F. "Rob" Falls, then president, if I would join the sixteen-person PRSA-Detroit board. I served on the board for twelve years through 2005. PRSA-Detroit represents about five hundred local public relations professionals from probably four hundred companies. The national PRSA has had as many as 20,000 members. Rob Falls established his own highly successful public relations agency in Cleveland for many years and remains a friend.

In 1997 while a board member, I presented a program to raise funds for student scholarships and chapter operations by establishing a corporate sponsorship program. I felt that if upstart JB&A joined as a full corporate sponsor, other public relations firms and corporations would too. Sharon McMurray of Comerica Bank and I were "first in" and others followed. It was, and is, a very successful program raising $20,000 to $40,000 annually. As of January 2013, the program has raised $428,000.

As you know, I believe in ethics in business, and to help promote this throughout our profession, I became the PRSA-Detroit's "Ethics Officer," a title I held for numerous years, so many that no one can really remember how many. During this time, not only did we support our national organization's effort to promote ethics, but we started our own program to have members annually pledge ethical business operations for themselves and their organizations. We hope that eventually the national PRSA follows our lead with a similar program. Hope Brown, then my colleague at JB&A, helped with this effort and did an excellent job.

By being members of and supporting PRSA, we also kept up with who was active and who looked like a strong professional. You never know when we might need to add someone, and what better place to look than our own professional organization.

Being active and supportive of PRSA-Detroit was a great way to continue to let people know how JB&A was doing. In the early years of JB&A, I would report on our progress at a board meeting. I could also ask if anyone knew of a young professional or more senior professional. This kept these industry leaders aware of who we were and where we were. In addition, my thought was that everyone has a favorite public relations firm that they might recommend that someone retain. I'd hope we could be number one on everyone's mind but being number two isn't bad either, especially if number one has a conflict.

I believe that the PRSA-Detroit membership was an important reason for our early success at JB&A.

I also have to thank Nancy Skidmore, the executive director of PRSA-Detroit for all her support over the years. She has been great for me and JB&A and PRSA-Detroit.

For the sake of PRSA-Detroit Chapter history, I must mention the Frank Seymour Cup. Frank Seymour was one of the first African American members of our chapter. I met him early in my career and knew he was a pioneer, strong public relations professional, and an outstanding golfer. He was also partner with my friend Gerald Lundy for several years in the 1970s before Gerald joined AMF, Inc. Frank was by far the best golfer in our chapter, and he donated the trophy that he frequently won to be presented to the winner(s) of the annual golf tournament.

The United States of America

I love our country. I wish I could give more to our country. We all need to pitch in and keep the United States of America as great as it is. We also need to always remember those who gave everything so that we can enjoy freedom. All I did was raise a family, build a career, and start and build a business. With the knowledge and experience I now have, I wish I could put it to use in Washington, DC. It is so sad to see what goes on there. Each party, each elected official, appears to make every single decision based on 1. What the party wants and 2. What decision will gain the most votes or lose the least votes? Many, maybe most Americans, think that politicians are afraid to "do what is right for the American people."

Politicians are not going to agree or like to see this in print, but let them ask their constituents what they think. And because of this decision process, compromise is lost in Washington, DC.

And honesty is also lost in politics. Where are the "honesty principles" of people like Abraham Lincoln and John Adams? Adams left a statement on the fireplace in the White House. It says:

"May none but honest and wise men ever live under this roof."

I wish I had more time to contribute to turning this situation around. But "We the People" can. So, let's do it. I'll participate as long as I am able.

CHAPTER 19

CAMP BAILEY

Why is our northern Michigan vacation home important? Because it helped me relax and see things clearly. Everyone needs a way to relax. I would go to this location in summer after a busy week, sit on my deck or around the fire pit, and make decisions that did not come clear during the rapid pace of the week, like opening the Lansing office, or which firm to merge with or not, or what to do about a certain associate. Several times I had conversations about mergers or acquisitions from my deck.

Camp Bailey is a great northern Michigan year-round home that is fifteen–sided, and called a pentadecagon. It is located 160 miles north of our home in Rochester Hills on a hill twenty-two steps above Floyd Lake, very near much larger Sand Lake. It is ten miles from East Tawas and Lake Huron—one of the Great Lakes that touch Michigan. The 160 miles can be easily driven in two and a half hours, so I could leave at 4 p.m. on a Friday and be relaxing on my deck by 6:30.

The one-acre lot has over one hundred trees and numerous rock gardens. I added a rock flow I named "river rock" that starts at the top of the hill near the house and "flows" or "winds" its way sixty feet down to the lake. Our home has over 2,200 square feet of decking, a wonderful fire pit, and a dock in the lake. What a relaxing place. It is a long way from my early days, and I am very pleased Janet and I were able to buy this wonderful place basically from funds earned at JB&A. We purchased Camp Bailey in late 1998 and paid it off in 2010. As Janet says, "When I take exit number 188 off I75, my entire attitude changes." I love the sound of the wind in the pine trees and the sight of the stars at night and the morning sun. I invite you to try rowing at dawn on our little Floyd Lake. Camp Bailey sleeps eleven people in beds and many others in cots. We have had as many as twenty-two to dinner. I decided against one of our early merger opportunities while at Camp Bailey and another time notified my family of the sale of JB&A while we all sat around the huge fire pit by the lake.

Janet began traveling to Sand Lake—located about one hundred yards from Floyd Lake—when she was in her twenties to visit her friend Helen Hasty. She returned many times over the years to visit Helen and her husband Willie at their cottage on Sand Lake. When Janet and I began dating in 1989, I went with her. At the time Helen was a "grand old lady" in her mid-sixties who had buried two husbands and a daughter but always remained cheerful and funny. Helen was a short woman who had gained some weight in her later years. She didn't look like she had two nickels to rub together, but she and Willie had built a multi-million-dollar estate. I always got a kick when someone would misread her and think she was a dumb little old lady. They would find out real quick how smart "Miss Helen"—as I called her—was.

Around 2002 Helen and her business partner in Michigan bought a piece of land in Western Lower Michigan for $200,000; Helen was the "bank" of the partnership. They closed on the deal one day and sold it the next day for $440,000.

Janet and I kept looking for a summer home we could buy to be near Helen, and in 1998 we found the home that became Camp

Bailey. It is not a cottage; it is our northern home and we do visit there year-round, but most often in the summer.

Helen spent summers at Sand Lake and winters in Lakeland, Florida. For years when I'd go up north on weekends, I would bring the week's collection of the *Wall Street Journal*. I would apologize that they were old, and she would say the information in the *WSJ* never gets old. When Helen passed away at eighty-three in 2010, she left us her small cottage that she and Willie bought in 1947. They added on to the cottage at least twice that we know of. It has a wonderful deck overlooking beautiful Sand Lake and is one mile by water to Camp Bailey and sleeps six in beds. We can now comfortably sleep seventeen people in beds. Helen left everything else in her estate to needy children in Polk County Florida through various organizations, but she knew the Bailey family could and would use her cottage. She was right; we use her cottage a lot and have named it, "Helen's Cottage or Hasty House."

Lessons Learned again: ***Remember to respect everyone. Appearances can be deceiving.***

Golf and Red Hawk

Golf is one of my hobbies. I can play some good shots and lots of not so good shots. But the pinnacle of my golfing career began in 2007 when I had the honor of playing the home of golf, "the Old Course" in St. Andrews, Scotland, along with three other wonderful courses in Scotland. Then in 2008 I attended the Masters Invitational at Augusta National, Georgia, and the PGA Championship at Oakland Hills, Michigan: two of the four major golf championships. I've also had the pleasure of playing four rounds of golf in Ireland at some of the finest courses there. But on July 29, 2011 came the ultimate for me. I had a hole in one on number 6 at Red Hawk while playing with grandson Tim Hansen. That is a memory that we will both share forever.

Red Hawk is an eighteen-hole championship golf course in East Tawas, Michigan, near Camp Bailey. It is carved out of the woods and the only buildings seen on the property are the club house and the home of the original owner of the property. Sometimes, if playing during the week especially, you can hear the silence and can see many animals, including deer, fox, and lots of other animals, and of course, red hawks circling in the sky. I've even seen an eagle. One spring there was a sign of a bear where it had sharpened its claws on a tree. It's a great design and very enjoyable. Let me know when you want a tee time.

Reading

Miss Morford, my high school English teacher, probably does know how much I love to read. And *you* know how much I love Mark Twain. I read *Huck Finn* and *Tom Sawyer* once a year and enjoy those books each time. But I read lots of other books too, as many as fifty a year. I try to mix in the classics with mysteries, with books about the old west, to US history, and especially Abraham Lincoln and WW II. And as you know, during my JB&A years, I also read many, many books on business, media, presentation training, and crisis communication. In 2013 I will only reach about thirty-four books read because of writing this book.

> Lesson Learned: ***Ongoing education is a must; it is sharpening the saw.***

Politics

At one time I thought about being a politician and once tried to join the Young Republican Club. But flawed candidates and blind support of issues and of those flawed candidates turned me off. Now I call Emily Gerkin Palsrok or Andy Hetzel to find out what is the behind the scenes thinking and to get my fix. But I follow it closely.

To many people's chagrin, I predicted the outcome of the 2012 presidential race even before the two conventions. I am an independent voter with Republican tendencies who has always voted for the person I believe will do the best job, regardless of party. I also believe that everyone has good ideas and therefore should be listened to. This also does not make for being a good "party man."

Religion

I don't go to church enough; maybe I can change that now. But I pray a lot. I pray for forgiveness, health, family, the ill and infirm, those who have predeceased us, and our politicians, hoping they will get things right; but most of all, I pray for family.

People

I've met a lot of people in my life. There was a time when I had never met a mayor, or council person, or a state representative. Those days are gone. I have met, and will enjoy meeting, many more in the years ahead.

CHAPTER 20

THE POWER OF OWNERSHIP

The Power of Ownership, indeed. Every day when I walked in the office and saw the JB&A sign in our lobby or traveled to Lansing and saw that sign, I was reminded about this very special thing I had created with Janet's help and then later with our associates. That was my name on the door. It was awesome. Those people worked for me...and they were building their careers at my company. I was encouraging them to challenge themselves to do more, always more, to better themselves. Even today when the name of my company has changed, the memory is strong. I hear from and meet with many former associates on a regular basis, and I am proud of what they have accomplished and what they will accomplish.

But "The Power of Ownership" is not just about a business. It is also about you and what you do with your life and career. You've got the opportunity to do the best you can so—do it. Make it happen for you and those around you. At JB&A we were doing things the way we wanted and had great plans for the future. JB&A was our company.

The management team would meet annually to discuss our company and individual area goals for the coming year. As I did for each year of JB&A—including and especially the first year—I ensured that the individual goals fit into our company goals. Then we'd proceed toward accomplishing those goals. These goals included budgets and staffing just like the company. Each person knew what they wanted to accomplish and each year began with the end of the year in mind.

We had opened an office in the state's capitol in Lansing, and no other Detroit-based public relations firm had ever been able to do that.

In the years up to 2008, JB&A had grown to be one of the largest privately owned public relations firms in the United States, reaching number 62 at our highest.

Our automotive, healthcare, and retail categories were ranked inside the top fifty in the United States. In 2002, 2003, and 2004, we were recognized as one of the Best Public Relations Agencies of our size to work for in the United States by one important industry source.

Our associate's morale was rated in the top five of agencies our size in the United States. Our clients—supported by us—had won more than one hundred awards of all kinds in those years, and we had won many ourselves for our professional services.

The JB&A annual payroll was more than $2 million, and in our best months we reached more than $500,000 in gross income…a long way from that $5,000 in our first month of business in 1996. The highest number of associates attained was thirty-two.

As I walked around the office listening to pieces of conversations, my chest burst with pride at the fine service we were providing our clients. And in so many cases, those conversations did not need me. It was a wonderful feeling.

To me, the power of ownership is not about the money. But you can make more money on your own for sure. The most I made before JB&A was $100,000 at Casey/Shandwick in 1995. In my best year at JB&A, I made about four times that amount—or—more per month than my high school goal of earning $20,000 annually. And I was able to put additional money in the 401K and savings. Plus, even in a tough economy, I was able to sell my company to an outstanding new owner who will keep our legacy alive, stay in Detroit, and be part of its future too.

To me, the power of ownership is about the people that I worked with at JB&A. They are family and I wish them the best always. Being a small part of helping them build their careers is like money in the bank to me. As I wrote this book, I reached out to about twenty-five current and former associates to gather facts and details and to get input from their perspective. Here is what one of them said to me in response to my request for information about her JB&A years:

> "I draw on our weekly company meetings, our management meetings, your individual mentoring of me, our annual brainstorming sessions and our coaching from Barry Demp all the time. It reminds me of the importance of communication and team work. I remember you saying there is no I in team. Did you include your list of success tips? I always admired how even in times when you may not have been treated the way you wanted, you never lowered your standards or ethics and were always the bigger person. You never burned bridges and always kept your anger in check even when you should have been beyond the boiling point.
>
> "I am looking forward to reading your book. Congratulations. You as always, are an inspiration."

This comment is worth more than money.

Being an owner gave me—and will give you—a platform to do so many other things, like contribute time and money to charities in the community, like contributing to not only PRSA but the Public Relations Student Society of America and the Wayne State University Journalism Institute for Minorities. I have included a list of what I call "Career Tips" that I used when speaking to groups of young professionals. We also gave it to interns and new employees at JB&A. It is true today and I believe it fits just about any profession and level, not just ours or beginners. I also got to play golf in some charity events too, which was a double benefit to me.

I believe now that if I had started JB&A when I left AMF, Inc. that it would have been a success. But I would have missed the Casey experience and all the people I met. I did this with my spouse's support…you can too.

I did learn though, that no one can have everyone like her or him. There are times when you must make decisions that some person will not like. All you can do is your best and what is right.

John's Awards

I am very fortunate and honored to have received and hopefully earned several awards in my career, all resulting from my and our efforts during the time of JB&A. I could not have won any award without the support of my family and the efforts and support of my JB&A family. I truly appreciate them all. The Wayne State University Communications Department Career Achievement Award is especially fulfilling as it marks my return to where I started after more than forty years.

1996 – PRSA Detroit Chapter Hefty Distinguished Service Award

1998 – Creatives for a Cure for contributions to Detroit's Creative Community

2002 – International Business Communicators Detroit–Communicator of the Year

2005 – Marketing & Sales Execs Detroit–Platinum Award for outstanding achievement

2006 – PRSA Detroit Chapter Hall of Fame Inductee

2012 – Wayne State University Communications Department Career Achievement Award

CHAPTER 21

THE NEXT BEGINNING AND CONCLUSION

What I have learned through my experiences and by observing so many others is that we all *can* achieve our maximum. It would be best to have a plan of action starting in high school, then college, and then in one's early career. But it can be done with or without an early plan—simply make a new plan. But you are the owner. Take ownership and make that plan no matter where you are. You can do it. I started JB&A when I was fifty-seven years old. It's never too late. Do not let someone else make news about you; make that news yourself.

To paraphrase something Abraham Lincoln said about owning a business in America that I believe:

"Some of you will be successful, others will be disappointed. Don't take it too much to heart, and better luck next time. To the latter I say, with renewed energy, begin again and make better luck next time."

People ask me how I am enjoying retirement. I've only changed jobs and am busier than ever. I am at a beginning. I am an author, and there will be more.

The financial charts say that at my age and because of my good health and routine, I should live another 23 years. I love spending time with Janet and my family, and I hope for that much more time with them at least. There are so many places to go: back to England, Scotland, Ireland, Europe, Africa, and more. And to see my grand-sons and great-granddaughter grow up.

When I pass on to my new world, I request a couple things. Oh sure, you can feel bad for a minute or two about losing dad, grandpa, husband, brother, friend, colleague, associate, favorite author, etc., but please, not for long. Remember: I never sat around. I have always tried to move to the next level and to do better at whatever I was doing. I could have done more for sure, especially if I had taken ownership sooner but when it is over, I hope you all can say: *"Well Done, John!"*

Lesson Learned: ***Luck is good. And hard work prepares you to take advantage of good luck.***

CHAPTER 22

YOUR CAREER TIPS

These tips for starting and building and maintaining a career worked for me and for many of the people I've been associated with over the years. Certainly they need to be adjusted to the person and expanded as time moves on, but the foundation will help anyone build a career.

- Work hard and work smarter! There is no substitute.
- Plan your stay on a job; discuss your plan with your supervisor.
- Don't stay on a job or in a position past your welcome.
- *Do* stay on a job or in a position until you have learned as much as you can.
- Learn as much as you can always. You own your career. Make it the best you can.
- Take each day and make something out of it.
- Network well and keep your network alive by keeping in touch.
- Learn the media—this is a separate network.
- Develop your strengths and improve your weaknesses.

- Work hard/Study/Learn/*Listen*/Grow. Get your professional certification.
- Be patient. You may be smarter than your boss, you will get there.
- Never say, "I can't," or "It can't be done." Most things can be done.
- Look for opportunities to be published, especially later in your career.
- Treat everyone with respect. Everyone.
- Practice liking people until you can do it genuinely.
- Never miss an opportunity to congratulate someone's achievement.
- Don't drink alcohol at client or customer events.
- Dress well and stay in good physical condition for you.

Steps to Consider as You Begin Your Business

I followed these steps as part of my plan at JB&A, and they worked for me. You will need to develop *your own* plan, but not doing one could cost you a lot of time, money, and/or business opportunities—or worse, loss of your business.

Know why are you doing this? If the answers are: I want to make money; I hate my job or my boss; I don't get paid enough; I want flexible hours…you are doing this for the wrong reasons and are likely to fail.

If the answers are similar to as follows: I'm passionate about this industry; I want to help people or companies; I want control of my life and to provide my family with a lifestyle they deserve…you will likely succeed.

- ❖ Determine what business you want to be in and have a passion for. Read and learn as much as you can on the subject. How are other firms in the field doing? Are they your competition? How much money are they making? What are their future prospects?

❖ Respect everyone always

❖ Know your strengths and weaknesses, strengthen each.

❖ Ask for help. Listen to outsiders. Their input can help you make important decisions. You don't know everything, listening to others helps you gain knowledge.

❖ Develop a business plan and mission statement. Share it with others to ensure you have thought of everything.

❖ Develop a marketing plan. How are you going to reach your potential clients or customers and engage them through social media, e-newsletters, etc. Marketing includes a sales plan and social media marketing plan. Think like your prospects to understand their needs.

❖ Consider working with an attorney and accountant as confidants in your early planning and to help set up your business. Not only will they provide their professional input, but they can provide an outside opinion for you to listen to.

❖ Select a name for your business that will make it easy for prospects to remember and that means something. Do not select a name just because you like it, like the name of your pet or hobby. If it's a horse farm, call it a horse farm.

❖ Develop a budget for the first year and break it down by month and by line item.

❖ Do not spend money until you have it. Warning: everyone does this, and I mean everyone. I did; read my book. If you don't need something, don't buy it.

❖ Always check with others to ensure you are not spending on something that can wait.

❖ Know your potential customers. List them by priority; hot, warm, long term prospects.

❖ Do as much advanced planning as you can. You can't do enough.

❖ Continue building on your network and keep it alive by staying in touch regularly by electronics and personal contact.

❖ Never assume anything. Let's say you have announced your new business to your prospects. Do not assume they saw the announcement or that they remember it; keep in touch with them. If you assume anything, assume they did *not* see your announcement or that they do *not* remember you.

❖ Begin each day with the end in mind. Know what you want to accomplish on a regular basis—even daily; certainly weekly, monthly, and annually.

❖ Know that you will lose business as well as win business. Don't let losing bother you, move on. This means that you must continue to prospect and look for new opportunities. Never assume you will get business until it has signed and agreed to work with you. Keep looking for more, always more. Once you stop prospecting it is hard to restart.

❖ Finishing second in a business presentation sucks for sure. But don't burn the bridge. If you remain positive, you never know, sometimes they come back to you.

❖ Speaking of burning bridges, never do this. Resist telling someone off. It is a small world. People move between companies and industries and can become prospects again.

❖ Manage your business. Know who you will handle finances, the books, paying taxes, getting your billing out on time. A well-run company serves its customer better.

❖ Establish realistic profit goals.

❖ Aim your marketing plan to reach target customers. Many business owners target a mass audience which wastes money and does not reach enough targets and costs too much. (Like buying an advertisement in a general newspaper or yellow or black pages phone book.) Develop a FAQ (Frequently Asked

Questions) worksheet and/or section on your website. Know your client's obstacles and be prepared to respond.

❖ Constantly evaluate your work so as to ensure you are making progress toward accomplishing your goals.

❖ Set timeframes for client responses and feedback. Don't rush them.

❖ Be creative. Look for different but economical ways to reach your customers.

❖ Brand your company. Know who you are and what you want to be and do not deviate from this. Stay consistent throughout the company with your brand message and your mission statement…especially in social media.

❖ Always do background checks. Hire slowly. Fire quickly.

❖ Always provide the finest quality work effort to your clients or customers. Your reputation depends on this. You can't over-service a good customer.

❖ Use publicity to your advantage. Announce new clients or customers. Announce anniversaries, financial successes, etc. This keeps your name in the papers, trade publications, and on social media, but most importantly, in front of your prospects.

❖ Keep pace with your growth. Don't add equipment or space or people before you need them. This is true for clients too. Don't add them if you can't handle them.

❖ Network well. Join organizations that will have your potential clients or customers as members. Do good work for those organizations. This adds to your reputation.

❖ Never stop looking for ways to do better, both internally and externally. Listen to what clients and customers say. Observe what others in your field are doing.

❖ Reinvent yourself. Constantly look for ways to improve everything you are doing.

CHAPTER 23

JB&A Associates—Special Recognition

I was fortunate to have worked with many amazing people at JB&A. I really could list almost everyone here, as so many did a fabulous job and contributed to our success. I saw so many young professionals join our firm and after a short time become really great public relations professionals. People like Daniela Petrovich Scholl, Lisa Gill, Kim Tassie, and Neil DeVries. But the following folks meant so much to JB&A and to me and our clients that I have to give them special recognition. In alphabetical order they are:

Amy Wilczynski: The consummate public relations professional. We always knew that Amy would do a professional job for clients and in new business presentations. She is very smart and helped so many of us do even better work for our clients. She has her own public relations firm now.

Andy Hetzel: Andy is one of the smartest people I have ever known. It was an honor to work with him. He is the person who came to me with the idea of starting a Lansing, Michigan, office, which we did under his leadership. He also helped build our health care business practice and is doing very well at Blue Cross Blue Shield of Michigan.

Beckie Thompson: I am the only person allowed to call her Becks. She joined JB&A out of the fashion industry and over several years became one of our best project managers and providers of public relations services to the health care field. She is a great media relations professional and my friend.

Beverly Mattinson: Some people say Bev was the best hire we ever made. She was controller for more than eight years and did a wonderful job. One time she and I were talking online with another firm about the possibility of our firms merging. Our outside consultant kept firing financial questions at both firm's controllers. Bev fired back with the answers because she had them, and the other firm's controller did not and thought Bev was trying to make them look bad. We knew we were not a fit.

Curt McAllister: Curt was the heart and soul of JB&A during his ten years. No one worked harder than Curt, and no one cared more about "the agency" than he did. When he started at JB&A, he wanted to learn the automotive media and later, all media. I gave him my counsel and told him when he knew as many media people as I did, that's when he had arrived. That happened in 2008. He is doing so well now at Toyota.

Debbie Reinheimer: Debbie was, and is, a great health care public relations professional. She added this expertise to JB&A and contributed to our firm gaining a strong reputation in health care. After several years with us, she joined our client, St. John Health, and we continued to work together. Debbie now has her own public relations firm.

Elizabeth Weigandt: E-Liz, as I call her, became one of the best media relations professionals on our staff. She chaired our NAIAS efforts for seven years and helped us set records for Rod Alberts and the NAIAS committee. She is a tireless worker, a great person, and my friend.

Emily Gerkin Palsrok: EGP, as I call her, was the first person we hired in our Lansing, Michigan, location to run the office. She is a Republican and is well respected by both sides of the aisle. Our Lansing office has been profitable in all of its more than nine years of existence. She is moving to a new and wonderful challenge and I know she will do well.

Frank Buscemi: A great guy and writer who became one of my closest friends. He'd rather be a rock band leader but is a great public professional while he "waits for the call." He and I are very close friends to this day and will be going forward.

Gayle Joseph: Gayle joined JB&A as a freelancer. We kept adding hours to her week until finally she became full time. She headed up many of our largest clients in the early years and helped develop our staff. She left for several years and returned to JB&A/LEA in 2011 to lead our Detroit office. We all welcomed her home.

Hope Brown: One of our longest serving associates, Hope is a wonderful writer and program developer. She has a creative flair that was welcomed on all accounts and within the company. I always knew that if I wanted an open and honest opinion on anything, and I often did, that Hope would provide just that.

Mary Ligon: I ran an ad seeking an experienced public relations pro. Mary, who was heading up public relations on staff at the North American International Auto Show, called me and said, "Hey, I want that job." We hired Mary and she performed fabulously well for years. She left to have a baby, then another, then another. I jokingly tell Mary she's on the longest maternity leave in history.

Michele Taipalus: I can't say enough about MT. She held us together in every way. When she joined us, she did not know much about computers. She learned in a hurry and became a very efficient technical person and kept us running. She was also my administrative assistant and sounding board to reality. She is now with LEA and is doing the same for them.

Michelle Culver: No one works harder than Michelle. She is almost always the last person to leave the office and then makes business calls on her way home. I could always count on her to do the best and most thorough job possible. Her accounts love and appreciate her and her work as I do.

Mike DeVilling: Mike was my number two guy for eight years. He is a solid public relations professional and great person. Everyone likes Mike. He was a team player for his entire stay with us and now has his own public relations firm. We are in touch, and I wish Mike and his family the best always.

Shaun Wilson: Shawn is a very strong public relations professional specializing in media relations. He has more contacts in the Detroit community than anyone. Shaun was my partner at Shaun Wilson & Associates Public Relations, a minority-owned public relations firm of which I was the minority owner. I am proud of our effort. He is doing very well at PNC Bank.

CHAPTER 24

JOHN J. BAILEY ORGANIZATIONAL HISTORY

Farmington Area Jaycees
Michigan Jaycees
Larkshire Elementary School PTA
Farmington Area Youth Soccer Club
City of Farmington Hills Parks & Recreation Commission
Public Relations Society, Detroit Chapter (PRSA)
International Association of Business Communicators, Detroit
   (IABC)
Detroit Press Club
Oakland County Business Round Table
March of Dimes
Detroit Regional Chamber of Commerce
Leadership Detroit
NAACP
National Press Club
Society of Automotive Engineers (SAE)
Adcraft Club of Detroit

Troy Chamber of Commerce
Automotive Hall of Fame
Woodward Avenue Action Association
Michigan Architectural Foundation
Detroit Institute of Arts
Detroit Zoological Society
WTVS, Detroit

CHAPTER 25

John J. Bailey Career History

<u>Burroughs Corporation — 1956 to 1969</u>

Mail clerk
Architectural Draftsman
Advertising/Public Relations Clerk
News Editor/*Burroughs B-Line* — International Internal Newspaper

<u>Chrysler Corporation — 1969 to 1970</u>

Mound Road Engine Plant — Plant Editor

<u>Batten Barton Durstine & Osborn (BBDO), Advertising & Public Relations Agency — 1970 to 1971</u>

Public Relations Representative

<u>PR Associates, Public Relations Agency — 1971 to 1972</u>

Account Executive

Thompson Brown Real Estate — 1973

Advertising & Public Relations Manager

Spinal Column Newspaper — 1974 to 1975

Publication Manager

Anthony M. Franco, Inc., Public Relations Agency — 1975 to 1989

Account Executive to Executive Vice President

Casey Communications Management/Shandwick, Public Relations Agency — 1989 to 1996

Senior Vice President to Executive Vice President

JB&A — 1996 through 2010

Founder, President and Chairman

Lambert, Edwards & Associates Public Relations · Investor Relations 2010 to 2012

Managing Director LE&A, Founder, JB&A

MY LIFE VISION

My life vision is for a peaceful and loving world where all people respect and honor each other…and all differences. Where people are encouraged—and supported—to be themselves in all ways. Where leadership and contributing to others are the foundations for a life of passion and purpose.

"No Legacy is so rich as honesty."

WILLIAM SHAKESPEARE

THE POWER OF OWNERSHIP
ACKNOWLEDGEMENTS

I have many to thank for helping me gather the facts and details for ***The Power of Ownership: How to Build a Career and a Business.*** Most importantly, my wife Janet who had to put up with me for the nearly two years this writing and producing this book. My family who I am sure I bored with stories about "the old days" and the 50 people from my past that I talked with about facts, details, dates and how they related to my story. I talked with many former Stroh executives and many former JB&A associates who not only gave me their input but their encouragement for me to continue the work.

My sister Beverly read the manuscript as did my son Craig, wife Janet and friend Ted Montgomery, himself an author and outstanding writer and editor. Thanks to them. My neighbor and friend Terry "Bear" Givens reviewed the book from a legal perspective and my daughter–in–law Susan provided technical input and helped me upload the files to the publisher numerous times.

And a special thanks to Dino Baskovic who has helped me with the marketing of the book on social media. He designed the website and has made me look to the outside world like I know what I am doing.

Thanks to the photographers who provided their work over the years. I tried and succeeded in locating some but not all of them. They all made valuable contributions. Note: Larry Peplin was the photographer who took my portrait photo.

And thanks to everyone, friends, family, acquaintances, associates and competitors that either directly or indirectly affected my career and helped me become the person I am.

www.ingramcontent.com/pod-product-compliance
Lightning Source LLC
Chambersburg PA
CBHW071413170526
45165CB00001B/263